Living In-Between

Living In-Between

Lament, Justice, and the Persistence of the Gospel

André Resner

WIPF & STOCK · Eugene, Oregon

LIVING IN-BETWEEN
Lament, Justice, and the Persistence of the Gospel

Copyright © 2015 André Resner. All rights reserved. Except for brief quotations in critical publications or reviews, no part of this book may be reproduced in any manner without prior written permission from the publisher. Write: Permissions, Wipf and Stock Publishers, 199 W. 8th Ave., Suite 3, Eugene, OR 97401.

Wipf & Stock
An imprint of Wipf and Stock Publishers
199 W. 8th Ave., Suite 3
Eugene, OR 97401

www.wipfandstock.com

ISBN 13: 978-1-4982-1739-2

Cataloging-in-Publication Data

Resner, André.

    Living in-between : lament, justice, and the persistence of the gospel / by André Resner.

    xii + 132 p. ; 132 cm. Includes bibliographical references.

    ISBN 13: 978-1-4982-1739-2

    1. 2. I. II. III. IV.

CALL NUMBER 2015

Manufactured in the U.S.A.   11/02/2015

For Christine Pfarr Resner

> . . . it befits a Christian to raise a protest against every form of senseless suffering, because it is contrary to God's will . . .
>
> . . . the only realistic hope a Christian can cherish, if he or she is not to succumb to despair, is the apocalyptic hope in God's eventual triumph over the power of death . . .
>
> —Johan Christiaan Beker, *Suffering and Hope*, 10

> . . . until all creation is renewed and all broken bodies healed true praise will never be divorced from lament.
>
> —Kathleen D. Billman and Daniel L. Migliore, *Rachel's Cry*, 109.

Contents

Permissions | ix
Acknowledgments | xi
Introduction | 1

    Part 1: The Apocalyptic Gospel, the Unfinished World, and the Tenacity of Faith: Meditations and Reflections

1 Rachel as Church: The Witness of Refused Consolation | 11
2 "Jesus Wept": The Longest Verse in the Bible | 22
3 Getting Our Hopes Screwed on Straight: Navigating Our Emmaus Road | 30
4 Breathing Prayer: Learning the Language of the Spirit | 40

    Part 2: Proclaiming God's Reign in a World that Is Passing Away

5 The Widow's Plight: Redefining Stewardship via Justice-Making and Justice-Keeping | 57
6 Casting Our Mammon on the Baptismal Waters: Preaching Economic Justice in Lent | 74
7 Preaching the Cross: A Personal Pilgrimage | 90
8 Lament: Faith's Response to Loss | 106

Conclusion | 125
Bibliography | 129

Permissions

All Scripture quotations, unless otherwise indicated, are taken from the New Revised Standard Version Bible, copyright © 1989, Division of Christian Education of the National Council of the Churches of Christ in the United States of America. Used by permission. All rights reserved.

An earlier version of the essay "Casting Our Mammon on the Baptismal Waters: Preaching Economic Justice in Lent" was originally published in *Journal for Preachers* 27 (2004) 42–50. Used by permission.

An earlier version of the essay "Jesus Wept" was originally published in *The Blue Rock Review* 1:1 (2005) 87–97. Used by permission.

An earlier version of the essay "Lament: Faith's Response to Loss" was originally published in *Restoration Quarterly* 32 (1990) 129–42.

An earlier version of the essay "Preaching the Cross: A Confessional Journey" was originally published in *Journal for Preachers* 24 (2001) 15–28. Used by permission.

An earlier version of the essay "Widow's Mite or Widow's Plight: On Exegetical Abuse, Textual Harassment and Learning Prophetic Exegesis" was originally published in *Review and Expositor* 107 (2010) 545–53. Used by permission.

Acknowledgments

FOR A SABBATICAL LEAVE in the fall of 2014, when I put most of these pages together, I thank the Board of Trustees, President Vergel Lattimore, Dean Trevor Eppehimer, and the Committee on the Faculty of Hood Theological Seminary. Hood Theological Seminary is a unique space for theological education, and I am grateful to have been given a place in its diverse mix. For a place to participate in and experience the *apocalypse* of the gospel at Hood, I thank the bishops, officers, and members of the AME Zion Church.

For colleagues in the Academy of Homiletics who have encouraged me, I especially thank Ron Allen, Jana Childers, Richard Eslinger, Stephen Farris, Mike Graves, Lucy Hogan, David Schnasa Jacobsen, Jim Kay, Stephen Johnson, Tom Long, Jennifer Lord, Barbara Lundblad, Alyce McKenzie, Henry and Ella Mitchell, Luke Powery, Robert Reid, Charles Rice, Clay Schmidt, Frank Thomas, Richard Ward, Maggie Wenig, and Paul Scott Wilson. Mike, I appreciate your wise counsel on some key matters that pertained to this book, and to our ministry of teaching and preaching. Our academy is a unique group of friends and I cherish the collegiality we share.

For the constant motivation to be the best human being I can be, and for forgiveness when I fall short, I thank our children: Tripp, Josh, Danny, Sarah, and Ana. For unfailing encouragement, I thank my father.

For a testing ground for the articulation of the apocalyptic gospel, I thank Cleveland Presbyterian Church.

For a contemplative space that provided the final push to complete this manuscript, I thank Jane and Mark Ritchie for their hospitality at StillPoint.

My students through the years have challenged me in and out of the classroom to "teach myself clear." I have always tried to make my classroom a safe space for students to grow and learn; I appreciate the reciprocity.

Finally, I dedicate this book to Christine Pfarr Resner, who shares my life and my love, and who believes in my voice, even when it makes her nervous.

Introduction

I HAVE A CONFESSION to make at the outset of this little book: I am not proud of what I am about to say about myself. I wish I could tell a different story here, but this is who I was, for better or worse. Mostly for worse as I think about it now.

I used to be a better salesman. It didn't matter what the topic or issue was. I would construct a way of perceiving it for my target audience, then lead them (I wrote "lure them" before getting a little anxious and editing "lure" to "lead") through the logic of my argument to a conclusion where they could see that my position was the best for them, the obvious choice. It's how I would trade properties in a game of Monopoly, move old furniture at a yard sale, negotiate a raise from my boss, or evangelize someone—yes, lead them to Jesus, help them receive the gift of salvation. Rarely did I question the connection between my talent to acquire Park Place in exchange for Reading Railroad and Illinois Avenue and leading someone through a maze of Bible verses and carefully organized questions so they would accept Jesus and be baptized by immersion right then and there, "just as the Ethiopian eunuch did in Acts 8 when he realized his need, and God's provision—'Look, here is water, what prevents me from being baptized?!'"

To me, the power of persuasion was just a neutral, special ability that could be used to win board games or lost people.[1] But every once in a while someone would force me to question such logic.

One older woman, who liked me very much, commented to me after my presentation to the church recommending an expansion to the

---

1. Augustine was the clearest and most persuasive advocate for using the ostensibly neutral tool of rhetorical persuasion to communicate the gospel so that Christian preachers would be more competitive in the marketplace of ideas and allegiances. See his *On Christian Doctrine* and my critique of his theory of rhetorical neutrality in *Preacher and Cross*. See also Marlin, *Propaganda and the Ethics of Persuasion*.

Introduction

sanctuary rather than going to multiple worship services, "You could sell screen doors to submarines." That worried me. And it started me thinking about the arrogance involved in using language to sway people to what I thought was best for them. It also got me to thinking about persuasion in relationship to the gospel.

Some have argued that the vast majority of human communication is persuasive discourse. In other words, most of what humans do in speaking is an attempt by one person to sway the other to his or her opinion or position. Because of this, the key question for human discourse becomes ethics, specifically, the ethics of persuasive discourse. Framed this way, the issue then revolves around the way our exchange of words affects those involved in the discourse. A crucial test for ethically virtuous discourse would be whether it respects the other and leads to ends that are truly best for the other, not just advantageous for the wordsmith.[2]

What does any of this have to do with the pages of this book? Quite a bit; in fact, everything. I've been asked by some who knew I have been putting together a book, "So, what's it about?" I've been uncharacteristically silent in response. Emails that ask go unanswered. Even my wife and daughter have become exasperated, pressing me repeatedly to tell them what I'm writing about.

I have been reticent, I suppose, partly because I no longer wish to participate in manipulative discourse. And so much of what passes for Christian preaching these days is just that. It sickens and saddens me.[3] Reticence cannot end in silence, however.

The pages here chronicle some of the ways that, over many years, I've come to understand the gospel, the Christian faith, the proclamation of the gospel, and the stewarding of the Christian faith in speech and action that the church is called to engage in. That does not mean that what follows is a "how to," not by any means. It is also not an "apology" in the classic sense of a defense of the faith. Some may even see it as the opposite of a defense. It is not a hostile attack on Christianity, but in some ways it is a protest, a seeming contradiction of the faith. It could be called a demonstration of nonconforming faith. But I am not organizing my words here to try to convince you that they are truer than more traditional versions of conforming faith. I don't think I am trying to convince; but if all, or even

---

2. See Lucy Hogan, "Preacher as Lover," in Reid, ed., *Slow of Speech*.

3. John Oliver has exposed the chicanery of some of America's televangelists on his HBO show *Last Week Tonight*. See https://www.youtube.com/watch?v=7y1xJAVZxXg.

INTRODUCTION

most, humanly exchanged discourse is necessarily persuasive, then I may be doing so whether I wish to or not.

My ethics in this discourse will be driven by two concerns. The first is my desire to respect and do right by my reader. I am not consciously selling anything here. The fact that this is a book, produced by a publishing house, and sold to the public, makes this claim a little awkward. But I didn't put the book together for commercial ends. And at this point in my career, I don't need a promotion or tenure. Rather, what I have tried to do is pull together in one place verbal and written utterances I have made here and there, on various occasions, and sometimes in the quiet of my own study, about what the gospel is and how I have wrestled with it in various biblical texts, as well as in the ups, but mostly within the downs, of my life. For it is in the downs of life where Christian faith is most fragile, most at risk.

Since the Christian faith is so much about life, whenever one has to encounter death one bumps into a contradiction, a challenge, and a threat to one's core beliefs and confession. I believe that we Christians have often lived in denial about the contradiction, have tried to out-shout the feelings of grief and sorrow with praise and thanksgiving. Many times this has only done damage to those who were truly in pain, grief-fully honoring the lives of those who were no more. I offer an alternate path here for those who feel painfully the disjunction between our confession of life and resurrection and our reality of suffering and death. I invite my reader to walk with me on this jagged journey that has been my own struggle to understand faith and the gospel while real life, and often turmoil and tragedy, is happening.

The second ethical concern that drives the reflections in this book has to do with the gospel itself, and my concern to, as best I can, be fair and true to it. Of course, "gospel" is a word that has had many variant meanings and associations attached to it. Indeed, even in my own faith journey, the faith of my childhood first rendered me a "gospel" that needed to be sold. The ultimate goal was to "close," and "win" the target with a confession of faith and a submission to baptism. The gospel was something to be obeyed more than received as a gift, much less something that reorganized all reality, including past, present, and future.

That early understanding of the gospel that the church of my childhood impressed upon me, I have come to believe, violated not only the first ethical concern stated above—respect for the other—but I now believe that it violates the gospel itself. The gospel that has come to relentlessly engage me, by God's grace, mercy, and persistence, and that I continue to wrestle with, especially in a world so filled with violence, terror, and death, is not a commodity to be sold to humankind, but a perspective, a construal, and a reshaping of reality centered in what God has decided to do and has accomplished in the death and resurrection of Jesus.

Most who would describe the gospel might say similar things, especially referencing Jesus' death and resurrection in some way. But even that does not resolve all questions; in fact, it raises questions. Because the meaning and significance of Jesus' death and resurrection is far from clear, and far from having a consensus of opinion in theological circles, whether academic, churchly, or popular. The point of departure and contrast here, though, pivots around several key questions: (1) What is wrong? (2) What is God doing about it? (3) What difference does this make? And (4) how will it all end? This is where the explication of the gospel as the Apostle Paul develops it, especially in its apocalyptic dimensions, is so important and maddening.

What is the basic outline of the apocalyptic gospel that Paul operated with, and out of? I will attempt a brief sketch here by means of the questions.

(1) What is wrong? Whatever the origin of the conflict, the world as we see it, and the cosmos that is invisible to our naked eye, is in a tug-of-war struggle between the powers of light and the powers of darkness, between good and evil, between what God made all things for and what those opposing powers have turned creation into. In a post-Holocaust world like ours, honesty demands that we posit that not everything that happens in this world is God's will. God is not a micromanager of the world's goings-on. Indeed, many have found it impossible to hold onto a position that asserts God as all-powerful and all-loving in face of a world and nature that is so violent and deadly ruthless. The apocalyptic perspective permits a position that holds to God as being all-powerful and all-loving; albeit that position must also posit that God has, temporarily at least, limited God's own response to many instances of suffering and violence. Why has God not intervened, when and if God could have prevented evil, violence, and suffering? That is one of the maddeningly unanswerable questions all humans face, but it is a particularly sticky one for Christians, who profess belief in a God that promises life, even abundant life. Suffice it to say that the reality of suffering demands a response—somehow, some way—from God.

(2) What is God doing about it? With the incarnation of Jesus, the coming into flesh of God's very own son, God initiated a search and rescue

INTRODUCTION

mission of God's created order. The four Gospels depict how unwelcome this initiative of God was to the powers that had wrested control of God's world. Resistance by the powers demanded a hostile takeover of a co-opted and broken creation.

The incarnation inaugurated God's New Creation. We see that unfolding inauguration of God's Reign in the Gospel accounts of Jesus' ministry of teaching, preaching, healing, and especially in his confrontation and conflict with the seen and unseen powers—notably incarnated themselves in the persons of the opposing religious leaders and the demons that inhabited and enslaved human victims, but also the human systems of oppression that Jesus confronts and begins to dismantle. It may be easier to see how governmental systems can embody means of human oppression, but the insidious nature of evil is that it worms its way into systems that appear on the surface to be of God, like the religious systems of the temple, synagogue, church, Christian school, seminary, and parachurch organization for human relief. They work their malevolence, only occasionally blowing up and revealing a contrary hand at work. In the person of Jesus as depicted in the Gospels, we see the God-man on the scene to "bind the strong man," by which Mark means Jesus' on-the-scene, deliberate disabling of Satan's deceptive and destructive work and way in the world, in religion, and in human lives and relationships (Mark 3:27). Maddeningly, however, the dismantling that is portrayed in the Gospel accounts has only begun, and is as yet unfinished.

(3) What difference does it make? In the Gospels we see what the world looks like with God in it. In the person of Jesus, wherever he goes, whatever he does, in his words and in his deeds, we see the Kingdom of God on earth in his person, work, and words. This is why wherever Jesus is, if there is someone who is ill, suffering, blind, deaf, or demon-possessed, that person is cured. It is as if the benefits and joys of the coming Kingdom of God have been poured out for a brief moment in this window of time that is Jesus' moment on earth. His presence and the power, released through his person, all inaugurate the dawning of God's New Day, God's New Age of shalom.

But that outpouring of God's Kingdom blessings is limited to the sphere of Jesus' own presence, and sometimes, by extension, the presence of those whom he has chosen and sent in his own name. This is why we see such a wild scramble wherever Jesus is. People scurry around to gather up all the sick and possessed and get them to Jesus, because this is their

5

Introduction

chance. Others try to position themselves in Jesus' path to get a glimpse or a touch, and when they guess right salvation—wholeness, health, healing, cure—comes to their house and person. Even the extension of Jesus' power proves effective through his apostles, those sent in his name and with his power to do his Kingdom-spreading work.

Sometimes, though, that power in Jesus' all-too-human emissaries proves temporary and transitory when, in one instance, they fail to remember where it comes from. This is certainly the message when Jesus' followers were unable to cure the suffering boy (demon possession? epilepsy?) at the bottom of the mountain where Jesus' was transfigured (Mark 9:14–29). The father brought his son to Jesus, but all he found was Jesus' disciples. They apparently took turns trying to heal the boy, but each failed, leaving a frustrated dad, a worse-for-the-wear boy, and an exasperated Jesus once he did show up. The scene could very well be a parable of the church in the world after Jesus's ascension, even up to the present day. A suffering world brings it wounded, weary, and tortured many to the church's doors, seeking the Jesus they have heard might be able to help and heal, but they find only us, his followers, and we not only do not and cannot bring the cure the world so desires, we make their condition worse. And God wonders how long he must put up with us.

Why does Jesus die? There are more than a few interpretations of the meaning of the death of Jesus in the New Testament and in the history of theological reflection through the ages. I do not claim to have the definitively clarifying answer to this question, but in the context of the apocalyptically construed gospel, Jesus' death, in conjunction with his resurrection, are at once a conclusion and a beginning. Those cataclysmic events are the consummation of an age of destruction and death and the commencement of the Age of shalom and life. In that newly inaugurated realm death is defeated, sin loses its grip, life is possible, and freedom from the powers of darkness is offered to creation and all its creatures.

But this is precisely where the exasperating part of the gospel comes in. Because in the New Testament narrative of this unfolding of God's long awaited and needed realm of Shalom, there is an interlude. God's dramatic play has gone to intermission.

As the Apostles' Creed puts it, "He ascended into heaven, and sitteth at the right hand of God the Father Almighty, from thence he shall come to judge the quick and the dead." What the ?!#@%! I say, come on, God, get

Introduction

on with it! Finish what you started, already! The early church said, "*Maranatha*, come Lord Jesus!" They meant the same thing.

Which leads us to: (4) how will it end? Important biblical scholars and theologians have noted the promise/fulfillment nature of the gospel. The gap between the one—*promise*—and the other—*fulfillment*—situates the Christian community in the period of waiting, hope, and faith. Each of those terms suggests incompleteness, and each also has counterparts: impatience, despair, and fear. Just as Jesus' ongoing followers exist between the poles of promise and fulfillment, they also find themselves precariously suspended between the poles of waiting and impatience, hope and despair, faith and fear.

A teacher and friend, Johan Christiaan Beker, in grappling with the elongated gap between the promise of God in Jesus' coming, death, and resurrection and the fulfillment of God in his return and final triumph in the consummation, calls this gap "the chronological embarrassment of the delay of the Second Coming . . ."[4] For all of Chris's own personal demons and struggles (he was carted off from his home in Holland and interred in a Nazi work camp during World War II), he nevertheless held on with the greatest tenaciousness of life and spirit to the Apostle Paul's vision of the coming triumph of God. No one that I know of sang louder in the choir of the apocalyptic gospel than Chris, and he used some arresting images to help us all imagine it and to stay strong and courageous in the midst of the embarrassing gap.

One such image (originally from Oscar Cullman by means of A. M. Hunter) comes fittingly from the inherently militaristic images that the apocalyptic struggle suggests. It is an image drawn from World War II.

> D-Day was but the prelude to V-Day, the Day of Christ, the parousia, the day of the final victory of God in Christ. It is the conviction that though the campaign may drag on and V-Day, the day of final glory may still be out of sight, D-Day is over and the powers of evil have received a blow from which they can never recover.[5]

Beker sees the death and resurrection of Jesus thus creating, to borrow a metaphor from grammar, "an ellipsis with two foci: the Christ-event and the Parousia, or the day of God's final victory. The dynamic tension between the two foci characterizes Paul's thought."[6]

4. Beker, *Paul's Apocalyptic Gospel*, 17.
5. Beker, *Paul the Apostle*, 159–60.
6. Ibid.

Introduction

What follows here are meditations, reflections, and essays that tease out the implications of this apocalyptic perspective on the gospel. In some you will see lament emerge as the language of honest, and sometimes even dissenting, protesting faith in the in-between-time struggle. In others you will see the lean toward justice-making as the actions of a community that attempts to put in place in the here and now what it knows God wants and wills, and what faith believes God will bring to bear in the soon-to-be-revealed Day of triumph. In others you will see me as preacher and teacher of preaching trying to imagine what the implications of the gospel, apocalyptically construed, are for preachers who wish to be faithful to God's revealed vision in Jesus Christ. My prayer is that any who grapple with the gap between what is and what will be may be strengthened and sustained, and in the end given courage to join the faithful protest against the powers of evil that, in their last dying gasps, continue to work against God's will and way. Joining the protest by the multiple means of (1) faithful lament, (2) unmasking the powers of evil in church and world, (3) establishing justice for the least of these among us, and (4) standing up to proclaim the truth of a Kingdom that remains frustratingly veiled, joins one to a work begun in Jesus, continued in Paul, and in every tear-stained saint through the centuries, until He comes.

PART 1

The Apocalyptic Gospel, the Unfinished World, and the Tenacity of Faith

Meditations and Reflections

PART 1

1

Rachel as Church:
The Witness of Refused Consolation

*(Meditation, Reflection, and Proclamation
on Matthew 2:13–23)*

The year was 77 of the new era. The place was Bethany, just outside Jerusalem. The Christians met there in a house that had belonged to Martha, Lazarus, and Mary. They had all died. But a brother in the Lord, Justus, had acquired the home and opened it to the other brothers and sisters, the followers of the Way. They gathered every first day of the week for prayer, breaking bread together, and sharing stories from Jesus' and the apostles' teaching, as well as their own lives of faith.

The group totaled about twenty—men, women, and children. Newcomers would sometimes join them as people moved to town or as others heard about them, became attracted to their way of life together, and their message about Jesus.

One new participant in the little community was an elderly Jewish man, Asher, who was originally from a small village near Bethlehem. He had only recently thrown his lot in with this group of Christians. He was still figuring out what his acceptance of Jesus as the Messiah would mean for him. That's why he was especially looking forward to the coming Sunday.

Word had gone out to everyone during the week that one of Jesus' original followers and apostles, Levi, the man who had formerly been a detested tax collector for the occupying Romans before Jesus called him, was going to be present. He was going to present a memoir of sorts from the time that Jesus had been with them.

Justus, Asher, and all the rest of them were living in the aftershock of Rome's attempt to eliminate the Jews, including the new Jewish sect that stubbornly insisted that Jesus was, in fact, God's Messiah in spite

PART 1—MEDITATIONS AND REFLECTIONS

of Rome's elimination of Jesus by execution on the cross. They insisted against all naysayers that God had vindicated this Jesus by raising him from the dead, thus inaugurating the New Age of God's Reign. It was a frustratingly bold word that begged many questions, the greatest of which was, "If Jesus is raised, then where is he now, and where is the evidence of this 'New Age'?" They kept insisting that the life of the community itself, emboldened by the risen Messiah's very Spirit, was the testimony to the truth of their message. Were the community to die, might the message die with them?

As the persecution persisted against the Christ followers, and as the first generation of eyewitnesses began to die off, there was increasing pressure on the old ones, like Levi (now known primarily as Matthew), to translate his own testimony from oral to written form before they died. Paul had been dead now for years. His letters circulated widely, and were copied in nearly every one of these ragtag faith communities in the empire. But now Matthew and a few others were circulating an entirely new testimony to Jesus, something that was being called the *euangelion*, the gospel, the good news about Jesus. It was another bold association, since *euangelion* was the word used to announce the birth of a new Roman emperor. It was as if Matthew and the others compiling these accounts were offering a counter-testimony to Rome's construal of the world, its future, and its true ruler.

When Sunday came, the brothers and sisters in the Lord made their way to Martha's old homestead. Each brought some food and wine for the worship and meal together. There was great excitement in the air as everyone anticipated Matthew's presence and his words.

When Asher arrived, Justus introduced him: "Matthew, this is Asher. He has just recently joined our group, professed his faith in Jesus as Messiah, and been baptized into our Lord. He is an eager learner." Matthew reached his arms around him and embraced him: "I'm glad I'm not the only old man here. Welcome, Asher. Did you ever see the Master when he was with us?" "No. Like everyone, I heard the reports of what he was doing—astounding stories! But it wasn't until the last year, when I got to know some of the brothers and sisters here, that I was drawn to him. I have been looking forward to your words, brother Matthew." Matthew smiled: "I am glad you're here."

After everyone had arrived, they sang a hymn from the Psalms. Someone led a prayer. Then Justus stood up. "We are grateful to welcome

Rachel as Church: The Witness of Refused Consolation

one who was himself with our Lord Jesus, one whom Jesus himself chose to be one of the twelve. Brother Matthew, we welcome you and are eager to hear what you have to say to us."

Matthew stood behind a table. Two others stood with him to help hold the scroll. "I am grateful to God to be with you today. Thank you, Justus, for your warm hospitality along with all who are in the name of our Lord Jesus, the Messiah. And it is good to be *here* again. It has been a long time. I remember fondly sharing meals in this room with Martha, Mary, and Lazarus. I miss them very much and know that in the coming resurrection we will all see their beaming faces alit with the light of Jesus' own face.

"I have brought you my gospel of Jesus the Messiah. I am particularly happy to read it in the very room where Jesus himself sat, ate, and taught. I have spent the past several years compiling it and I pray that it will bless you who hear it. I have read it to my church in Antioch of Syria. They urged me to share the words in all the cities and villages where there are people like you, eager to hear the gospel of Jesus the Messiah, the son of God. These are difficult days. It appears that the Roman Empire threatens to exterminate us. But I want you to be assured that it is only an appearance. The power they wield is temporary. It cannot prevail against the Kingdom of Heaven, which Jesus himself inaugurated in his resurrection. As our Lord Jesus often would say when he taught us, "Let those who have ears to hear, listen!"

His eyes travelled toward the scroll and he put a finger on the first word. "An account of the origins of Jesus, the Messiah, the son of David, the son of Abraham." Asher listened intently. He shut his eyes and remembered the stories attached to each of the names in the genealogy. It warmed his heart to hear the names that he had known his whole life: Isaac, Jacob, Judah, Boaz and Rahab, Boaz and Ruth, David and Uriah's wife, Solomon, Josiah, all the way to Joseph and Mary. It was a checkered history, witnessing to the grace and providence of God to keep working through fallible human beings to accomplish God's purposes in the world.

He told of the miraculous birth—Jesus, Emmanuel, God with us. And of King Herod, the tyrannical Roman puppet king. And the Magi—astrologers, readers of the stars, feared and ridiculed men. Itinerate predictors of the future. They were Gentiles, these Magi, yet they were in Jewish territory, seeking a new Jewish king, and somehow gaining an audience with the apparently soon-to-be-former Jewish king, Herod, and giving him the startling news in the form of a question: "Where is the child who has been born *king of the Jews*? For we have observed his star at its rising, and have come to pay him homage" (Matt 2:2).

They, here to worship a *Jewish king*? And here they stand in the presence of the Jews' king, Herod, clearly not worshipping him, but rather asking him for directions as if he were a gas station attendant, "Hey, you know how to get to the new Jewish king, Mr. Herod, the old Jewish king?" Herod, Matthew told them, was quite disturbed by their inquiry, and all Jerusalem with him.

All proceedings in the palace ground came to a standstill as Jerusalem's brightest and best assembled to determine where the Messiah was supposed to appear. Eventually there was a consensus: Bethlehem. So Herod, putting on his best poker face, called the Magi back and asked them where the star first appeared. "Then he then sent them to Bethlehem, saying, 'Go and search diligently for the child; and when you have found him, bring me word so that I may also go and pay him homage'" (2:8).

The Magi went. They found Jesus, and they worshipped him. But they did not go back to tell Herod. They were warned in a dream to bypass Herod on their way home. Joseph too was warned in a dream to get out of Bethlehem ASAP because the enraged Herod was about to wreak havoc there in an attempt to kill the rival baby king.

And then Matthew read this:

> When Herod saw that he had been tricked by the wise men, he was infuriated, and he sent and killed all the children in and around Bethlehem who were two years old or under, according to the time that he had learned from the wise men. Then was fulfilled what had been spoken through the prophet Jeremiah:

> "A voice was heard in Ramah,
> wailing and loud lamentation,
> Rachel weeping for her children;
> she refused to be consoled, because they are no more."
> (2:16–18)

Matthew paused, looked up from his scroll across the room, and saw Asher, no longer reclining on the floor but standing, brow wrinkled, mouth pursed, looking away. He slowly turned his head and looked around the room at everyone, his eyes swelling with tears, rage, and bafflement. Matthew asked him, "Asher, friend, are you all right?"

Rachel as Church: The Witness of Refused Consolation

Asher looked back at Matthew, "So that's what happened." His voice, barely audible, trailed off as he walked to the window, put both hands on the sill and leaned toward the opening, looking down. The room was still, all eyes fixed on Asher. "What happened, Asher?" Matthew implored.

"I was a young boy, running back and forth through the freshly washed clothes that my mother was hanging out to dry in the warm air. Suddenly everyone turned and looked at what appeared to be a sandstorm to the north. But soon we heard the roar of horses at full gallop, carrying soldiers. They wore battle gear, gleaming breastplates, and helmets, and their swords were drawn. Others had spears. We looked around, wondering where the opposing army was that they were about to adjoin in battle. But we could see none.

"And then we saw who the enemy was. It was the children." Asher paused, clenching his eyes shut, then said, "They swept through the town killing all the little children. Mothers frantically snatched up babies and ran with them clutched to their chests. Soldiers dismounted and chased them, running their spears through baby and mother. My mother quickly wrapped me up in clothes on the ground and told me not to move or make a sound. She ran for the house, but two soldiers were already coming out. She rushed in and I heard her screams. My brother and sister had been slaughtered."

He turned and looked straight at Matthew. "In a matter of minutes it was over. Every house had been rampaged. Blood flowed through the streets. Mothers and fathers wailed, carrying their newly dead children in their arms, holding them up to the sky, screaming "*Why?!*" to a silent heaven. We watched as the sandstorm rode off to the south. We would later learn several towns in our area had suffered a similar fate.

"Our village was devastated, destroyed. It never recovered in all the years I lived there. It felt cursed. I never remember my mother smiling after that day . . . I always felt guilty being the one who lived, who survived. I hated the soldiers, and Rome all the more. I considered becoming a Zealot when I was a young man, to avenge the children's senseless deaths."

Asher's face hardened and his tone gained momentum. "But now, I am confused. On the one hand, it seems that I should hate Herod, who was the one who dispatched the soldiers because he was afraid of being displaced by the new king. But you, you have made it even worse.

Because that new king that he feared was Jesus . . . and his fear of Jesus was what dispatched the soldiers . . .

"*And*, you tell me that the Gentile Magi got a dream, and escaped. You tell me that Joseph, Jesus' father, got a dream and escaped. But you don't tell me why my father didn't get a dream, get a warning, get a chance to escape, a chance to see his children grow up. Why did I have to grow up an only child with two parents destroyed by grief?"

Getting more and more agitated, he pounded both fists against the sides of his head, "This is the worst story I have ever heard! You want me to believe in a Messiah that was spared at the same time that a horrific slaughter in numerous towns in and around Bethlehem was permitted? You are asking me to be awestruck that God can impregnate a virgin yet cannot keep a paranoid, power-crazed king from killing innocent children?" Raising his voice even louder he said, "Tell me, Matthew, how can this be *euangelion*, good news?!" He slowly crumpled to the floor and grasped whatever dirt he could from the floor and put it on his head. Stunned, everyone looked to Matthew.

Matthew took his hands off the scroll, went across the room and sat on the floor next to Asher, placing one hand on his shoulder. Asher looked up at him. It was Matthew who was now weeping. Just then both men fell into each other, embraced, and wept. They kept weeping with loud wailings while one by one the others gathered around them and laid their hands on them. Many joined in the weeping and wailing.

There at the home of Martha, Mary, and Lazarus, where Jesus in-the-flesh had supped, where this fledging little church gathered to worship the risen Christ, trying against all odds to say that in them the Kingdom of Heaven had taken up residence on earth—there was Rachel, again, wailing and lifting up loud lamentation, refusing to be consoled, because her children were still no more.

Rachel is the church, present in the world to voice in her weeping the necessary protest against death, loss, the cessation of what God wills and wishes to be. Rachel, the church of the risen Christ, stands over against every power that negates life, every force that extinguishes the breath of life that God breathes into humankind that it might live.

Rachel as Church: The Witness of Refused Consolation

There she was, Rachel, huddled in a little home where two sisters had once wept for their dead brother until Jesus came to town and, through tears of his own, raised him from the dead. There, in the shadow of a Roman Empire that was attempting to wipe her off the face of the earth, was Rachel weeping in protest of the dead, in the face of a promise of life that always seems impossible to grasp in the presence of slaughtered innocents.

The weeping for senselessly slaughtered children never ceases. It cannot cease. It must not cease. Premature consolation for devastating, absurd loss must always be refused. Nothing in the story of the gospel covers it up, makes up for, or explains adequately enough the loss of the innocents. It doesn't matter if Rachel's cries make many nervous—"Who will come to the Christmas play if that scene's in there?" As Christopher Morse puts it, "her refusal [of consolation] is honored in the Gospel as faithful testimony."[1]

The contemporary church commits a crime—indeed, it opts out of its true identity—I believe, when it tells Rachel that she's wept enough, that she needs to "buck up and get back to praising; after all, Jesus has been raised so we can put away our tears!"

No. There is a witness in wailing, loud lamentation, and refused consolation. And strangely enough, it is a witness to the *resurrection*. To silence the wailing, the lamentation, and to force consolation before the time, would strangely be to silence the resurrection witness.

As Morse again states, "By not believing *any* consolation short of God's own descent into hell in Christ, the refusal of Rachel becomes a faithful witness pointing to the resurrection."[2]

Some people, uncomfortable with the Rachels among us who weep in grief, believe they continue their weeping and their grieving because they don't believe in the resurrection enough. "If Rachel just believed more, or enough, in the resurrection, she wouldn't be so sad." Nicholas Wolterstorff wrote in the aftermath of his own son's death:

> Elements of the gospel which I had always thought would console me did not. They did something else, something important, but not that. It did not console me to be reminded of the hope of the resurrection. If I had forgotten that hope, then it would indeed have brought light into my life to be reminded of it. But I did not think of death as a bottomless pit. I did not grieve as one who has no hope. Yet Eric is gone, here and now he is gone; now I cannot

---

1. Morse, *Not Every Spirit*, 10.
2. Ibid., 11. Emphasis added.

talk with him, now I cannot see him, now I cannot hug him, now I cannot hear of his plans for the future. That is my sorrow. A friend said, "Remember, he's in good hands." I was deeply moved. But that reality does not put Eric back in my hands now. That's my grief. For that grief, what consolation can there be other than having him back? . . . Though I shall indeed recall that death is being overcome, my grief is that death still stalks this world and one day knifed down my Eric. Nothing fills the void of his absence. He's not replaceable. We can't go out and get another one just like him.[3]

The language of lament is honest language in the face of suffering and loss. And of all people in the world, we must be honest—we Christians, whom the world must think are delusional because we so often turn a blind eye, a deaf ear, and a seemingly uncaring heart away from the very real suffering, senseless loss, and injustice in our world. We are rightly accused of denial and triumphalism whenever we refuse to "weep with those who weep," so we can instead disjointedly praise, or worse, attempt to shame those who weep and grieve as being "short on faith."

No, we must be honest, and that's where the specter of Rachel helps us out, even gives us a new image for the church in a world as violent as ours is. Because our world weeps today—in Darfur, the Middle East, Iraq, Afghanistan, Panama, in Haiti and the Philippines, in Bangladesh, in Senegal, in Zimbabwe, in Ferguson, Charleston, New York, Chicago, and Los Angeles—and the church, rather than sitting on the ash heap, embracing today's Rachel and weeping with her, often looks the other way, passes by on the other side, contrives smiley faces and false happiness in the face of the world's tears, whips itself into a frenzy of premature celebration, and in some cases even makes up a "gospel" of greed and markets it as "blessing," "prosperity," "enlarged borders," and all the while mocks this world's starving, wounded, and those hopelessly sinking into increasing debt created by predatory creditors, and offers them false hope, always with a lowercase "h." If the prosperity gospel preachers and the miracle cure preachers are right and true, shouldn't they be spending most of their time in Africa, Afghanistan, Nepal, and Haiti rather than megachurches and former sports arenas in major U.S. cities? We keep whitewashing tombs, denying the decay within.

Rachel, weeping and refusing consolation, is an Advent story of the dark side of Christmas. It reminds us that the cross looms over the stable

---

3. Wolterstorff, *Lament for a Son*, 31.

Rachel as Church: The Witness of Refused Consolation

and the manger. Martin Luther said that it is in Rachel's cries that the Nativity and Good Friday come together.[4] Rachel's refused consolation reminds us that though the light shines, it shines in a darkness that threatens to overcome, if not the Light itself, at least all the rest of us whose tears threaten to blind us to that Light.

The lectionary does not like this story. It plops the episode onto the second Sunday in the season of Christmas, year A, the Sunday after Christmas, traditionally known as "Associate Pastor Sunday." But preachers generally observe the "Passover" on this text and do not preach from it. Most deem there to be no "preachable X" in this sad tale.[5] There are no Christmas pageants that choose the slaughter of the babies over the adoring Magi or the shepherds. I see preachers and parents skip it when reading Matthew to children. We sense an "R" rating on this text due to graphic violence, and slyly turn the page before the child senses we are skipping part of the narrative. There has in all likelihood never been a children's sermon on Herod's slaughter. The Jesus movies edit it out as too traumatizing. Not even Matthew gives us a moral to tease out of it, or an excuse.

It is what it is. Horrific. Tragic. Disgusting and disturbing—just as our unfinished world is. It is theologically maddening. No other Gospel writer decided to include it. We have to resist our urge to pick up the remote control and change the channel to the Lucan Network where they're broadcasting a buoyant Christmas musical at this very moment, complete with full orchestra, happy angels in bright choir robes, and live, docile animals lying around on the stage.

Even at the risk of alienating a hearer or reader, even someone who knows what it is like to have a child ripped from one's arms to die unnecessarily, Matthew is saying, "the story of Jesus is tragedy as well as comedy, even as it is fairy tale."[6] Before the gospel can be the best news that we have ever heard, it is the worst news that ever was. Matthew's story does not do away with bad news. Instead, like a cold slap in the face, it testifies to the fact that the gospel forces some of the worst behavior that humankind is capable of. T. S. Eliot wrote, "Humankind cannot bear very much reality."[7] Instead it prefers lies, thin veneers of comfort, and distractions layered blindingly over the hard truths of this world's sorrow.

---

4. Morse, *Not Every Spirit*, 11.
5. Farley, *Practicing Gospel*, 77–78.
6. Buechner, *Telling the Truth*.
7. Eliot, *Four Quartets*.

PART 1—MEDITATIONS AND REFLECTIONS

The gospel will not have it so. Matthew reminds us, that even as we anticipate the joy that Jesus' coming into this world signifies, we must not forget that the yawning gap between his first coming and second coming has allowed Rachel's wail to resound with greater and greater echo because of all the suffering that remains unaddressed. If the blood of just one man, Abel, had the power of voice in the divine ear, voice to cry out to God from the ground seeking . . . what? Justice? Vindication? Consolation? If one man's unjustly spilled blood had that power of voice, what must the chorus of all those who have joined him at the hands of their brothers sound like in the ears of our heavenly Parent?

"Maranatha! Come, Lord Jesus! Bring a resurrection vindication long overdue to all the Rachels whose eyes swell and whose backs ache under the weight of their grief. Hear our cry as intercessory prayer. Hear our refused consolation as a defiant faith in the promised resurrection. We do believe; help our unbelief!"

Matthew and Asher wept for a long time. After a while Asher leaned back and wiped his face with the back of his hand. He looked Matthew in the eye and said in a voice at once soft and strong, "You must keep telling it. Not because it makes sense of anything. It doesn't make sense of my brother's and sister's deaths, nor of all my friends' and neighbors' deaths that day. You must tell it because, strangely, mysteriously, it *is* part of the gospel. Jesus was spared that day, only to be slaughtered another day by another would-be ruler, a pretender. No one ultimately escapes the injustice of another miscreant in this world. The gospel is the horrible news that when God enters the world, this world's powerful are so threatened that they scramble their resources to try to thwart God's plans. The gospel is not that God spares the lives of a few people here and there by using dreams and angels. The gospel is that if this one named Jesus does not die on the cross for us and be raised by God, then no one has any hope that the scapegoating or the violence will stop, and be replaced by resurrection and life."

Asher continued: "If I understand the gospel, I believe I will see my brother and sister in the resurrection. And I will see my mother and father, finally smiling, and I will even see Rachel—*Rachel finally consoled*, for her children are now alive forevermore, never again to be threatened by *temporary* power or *temporary* death. Go on, Matthew, keep telling

Rachel as Church: The Witness of Refused Consolation

your story, your gospel, your testimony of Jesus. Keep telling the truth of it, even when it breaks hearts in two. For God's wholeness can only be truly experienced as good news when it confronts the truly broken. The gospel is truly gospel not because it avoids the worst of our lives, and the worst of the human condition, but precisely because it plants itself squarely in the middle of the worst of it all."

Matthew embraced Asher one more time and whispered, "I'm so sorry." He wiped his face, walked back across the room and found his place in the scroll. Everyone settled back into each one's place. Asher closed his eyes again and Matthew read, "When Herod died, an angel of the Lord suddenly appeared to Joseph in Egypt and said, 'Get up, take the child and his mother, and go to the land of Israel, for those who were seeking the child's life are dead.' Then Joseph got up, took the child and his mother, and went to the land of Israel."

This meditation is for all of the children whose lives have been senselessly cut short, to all the parents, brothers, and sisters who grieve their loss, and for all those who wait impatiently holding vigil. It is for all who, like Rachel, stubbornly, faithfully refuse cheap and temporary consolations and hold out instead for God's promised *resurrection consolation*. It is for the church in our violent world today—Rachel, holding the vigil of lament until he comes. "Maranatha, come, Lord Jesus."[8]

---

8. See also the excellent resource by Kathleen Billman and Daniel Migliore, *Rachel's Cry: Prayer of Lament and Rebirth of Hope.*

2

"Jesus Wept": The Longest Verse in the Bible

(Meditation, Reflection, and Proclamation on John 11:35)

LAZARUS CAME FORTH. BUT what about the next day? Did he no longer have that lower back pain after his resurrection? He came forth to die yet again. And there was no Jesus around to raise him the second time. Mary and Martha had to go to their brother's funeral twice, unless he was raised only to grieve at their funerals first.

What do you say at someone's second funeral?

The heart yearns. It yearns in the gap between the gnawing ache of our experience in the world and the dream of the promise. The brokenness is sometimes all that we can see and feel.

I wish I could fix these glasses. My fourteen-year-old son bought them. He spent ten of his own dollars on these cool-looking pink-lensed and tortoise-rimmed sunglasses. Then he left them on the floor of his room. A shirt got tossed on top of them. He stepped on the shirt, and the glasses, and the right arm was severed off at the hinge. It's a clean break but the glue will not hold. They are broken and cannot be fixed. He does not have many ten-dollar bills. He really wanted these glasses. He had them about two weeks before the accident.

He brought them to me and said, "Dad, can you fix these?" In his voice was disappointment, anger, frustration, yet hope that I might be able to do something. He's seen me fix things that he thought were unfixable before.

I worked with them. It seemed that so much was at stake. More than the ten dollars. More than the cheap sunglasses.

It's been three months. I still have them on my desk. I still want to fix them. To restore them to wholeness and functionality. To see him happy to have them back on his face, looking so cool. To reverse the frustration.

"Jesus Wept": The Longest Verse in the Bible

To redeem the ten dollars. To restore his trust and confidence in me as his dad. Why do I keep trying to fix these sunglasses? If I keep failing will he someday stop bringing me broken things to fix?

Is this why we eventually stop praying? Stop expecting?

I read Rabbi Charles A. Kroloff's sermon "*Tikun Olam*."[1] The Hebrew title means "To Mend the World." The assumption is that there is something broken, something dreadfully askew, with the way the world currently is. The task of God and humankind in the midst of this brokenness is reparation. The preacher insists that there is a divine-human cooperation in addressing and remedying the world's brokenness. That reparation is the faith community's chief mission, joining God in active restitution.

Bob Dylan wrote pointedly about the cumulative brokenness of even ordinary American experience:

> . . . Broken bodies broken bones
> Broken voices on broken phones
> Take a deep breath, feel like you're chokin'
> Everything is broken . . .[2]

And then there is the tape that plays in my mind. I don't know where it came from, but it mocks me:

> The only way to make it in this world
> is to close your eyes
> to harden your heart
> put your head down
> and just bull forward.

Yet, we humans are constitutionally too fragile to sustain the bull charge. Too fragile for a lifetime of hardness of heart. All the pain, disappointment, and imperfect love that is our experience accumulates like plaque in the arteries. There is no statin for the cholesterol of hate, violence, resentment, unforgiveness. This is why we need our numbing agents, and why our numbing agents fail us. They only temporarily blind us to the broken world, and then there's the morning and the new bad news of the day sitting on our doorstep. This is why the s/Spirit yearns for *Tikun Olam*.

In the story that John tells in the eleventh chapter of his Gospel, Lazarus came forth to a second life because Jesus wanted to make a point about resurrection and himself. He let Lazarus die when he could have prevented it.

---

1. Kroloff, "*Tikun Olam*," in Resner, ed., *Just Preaching*, 101–5.
2. Bob Dylan, "Everything is Broken" (Special Rider Music, 1989).

PART 1—MEDITATIONS AND REFLECTIONS

Before getting to Bethany he looks quite calculating. He stalls long enough for the sick Lazarus to die, "so that the Son of God may be glorified through it" (John 11:4). From a distance it probably seemed like a good idea. Then they arrived just outside Bethany.

Lazarus had been dead four days. The town was in deep grief. Lazarus' sisters had sent word to Jesus days before, asking him to come help their sick brother, whom they knew Jesus loved. Now Jesus saunters to the edge of town and their grief is compounded. How could he have delayed coming? They heard Jesus was there and Martha went out to see him. But Mary didn't. Not then. Not yet. Could she not yet face him?

Martha confronted Jesus: "Lord, if you had been here, my brother would not have died." Mary then came out to him and said the same thing: "Lord, if you had been here, my brother would not have died" (John 11:21, 32). Both sisters were weeping. Their friends who had come out with them were weeping too.

All calculations aside, Jesus' own heart was breaking.

But why? He was there as the self-professed "resurrection and the life." He was there knowing what was about to happen. Lazarus would be home that day, raised from the dead and alive. Why should he weep? He had the trump card that would overturn all the hurt they felt. He might have just said, "Don't worry yourselves so much. Everything's going to be all right. Just wait and see."

Lots of people say this kind of thing when we're experiencing void and despair, but we know they don't really know what they're talking about. They're usually just trying to avoid our grief and anguish as well as their own experience of brokenness because it just plain hurts too damned much.

Jesus is the one guy who could say, "It's all going to work out all right," and really mean it, really back it up. But he never does. Facing the grief that these people feel, he feels it too. And standing there in the midst of their turmoil, questions, accusations, bereavement, and crying eyes, "Jesus wept."

John 11:35. I learned it as a child as the answer to a trivia question: "What's the shortest verse in the Bible?" Answer: John 11:35, "Jesus wept." It was one of many trivia tidbits I knew about the Bible. The longest verse is Esther 8:9; the longest chapter is Psalm 119; the shortest chapter is Psalm 117; and on and on . . .

I used to stare at John 11:35 amazed at its economic terseness. *"There it is: the shortest verse in the Bible—can you believe it?"*

"Jesus Wept": The Longest Verse in the Bible

In my childhood Bible I wrote inside the front cover, "John 11:35, Jesus wept." It's the only thing I wrote in that Bible given to me by my grandmother July 21, 1965, when I turned eight years old. John 11:35 is the only verse in that Bible that I completely circled with pencil.

It never disturbed me then. It was nothing more than a Jeopardy answer.

I didn't know then what it meant to really lose. I didn't know what it meant to grieve the loss of someone I loved. Someone who up to that point in my life was a major ingredient in the way that I defined my own being. Someone without whom my own self-definition would be immeasurably diminished.

No Lazarus had left this Martha back then.

Now I can't read it without my own eyes welling up. I am fifty-eight years old now and have through the years lost so much and so many that meant so much to me. Senseless deaths and severances. A virus here takes my son. An infection there takes the woman who had become my mother in Christ. A cancer cell multiplies in my best friend's body and sweeps him away. Misunderstanding takes a friend. Lies take another. Political correctness takes yet another. Fundamentalism? There goes a whole room. My birth mother dies. Relationships that mean the most to me become strained to the breaking point. I feel out of control to bring about the peace that I most want.

"Lord, if you had been here..."

Jesus wept. He wept because their hearts were broken. He wept because they wept. He wept because Lazarus was dead and it had rocked the world of everyone that knew him. He wept even though he stood there as "the resurrection and the life." In his weeping, the Resurrection wept. Life wept. The Way wept. Truth wept.

Was the lesson in resurrection worth the pain of their brokenness? In the moment standing there with them before they were even at the tomb, I wonder if he wished he had written his lesson plan for this teaching moment differently.

They arrived at the tomb. John vividly describes Jesus' reaction upon arriving face-to-face with the cave and the stone in front of its entrance. John uses the word *embrimomai* to describe Jesus' feelings, a word that was used in the ancient world for the angry snorting of horses. It's a word that is used elsewhere in the New Testament when someone is said to sternly order someone. It's a word that has to do with abject anger. Though every context other than John 11 suggests the semantic core of this word has to do with anger, frustration, and indignation, I could find only one translator who dared translate the John text in this way. Eugene Peterson tried to get the edgy meaning of the Greek word across in his translation of *The Message*: "Then Jesus, the anger again welling up within him, arrived at the tomb" (11:38). If a director were advising his actor how to portray what this looked like, he might say something like, "When you see the closed tomb of your dead friend, shake your head vigorously side to side while snorting in a deep guttural tone. Remember, you are coming up against that which you have come into this world to defeat—this is your head-to-head in the cage with the last enemy."

Jesus, the self-proclaimed resurrection and life, couldn't help but be his angriest in a graveyard. Especially in front of the grave of a close friend whom he loved. Everything that the graveyard said and stood for was a challenge to his very identity. If he was who he said he was, a grave would raise a question mark every time it was filled. Each tomb, each marker, mocked him as he walked by them. Every etched-in-stone end-date to a person's life cried out to him as he passed, "*Liar!*"

Jesus wept. And he was angry, again. However we translate this, it seems clear that anguish and anger are fixed onto one another here and reverberate throughout the scene of Jesus with Mary, Martha, and the crowd, both before and at the tomb. And that anger and grief reach perhaps the sharpest focus in the accusatory statement that both sisters had levied against him: "Lord, if you had been here, my brother would not have died."

And do we not feel the same way, but just haven't had the guts to say out loud that hard and accusatory truth? "Lord if you had been in the heart of Africa, twelve million people would not have been stolen from their homes and communities for the slave trade." "Lord, if you had been in Nazi Germany, you could have stopped Hitler before he began." "Lord, if you had been in Indonesia, your mighty and outstretched hand could have stopped the Tsunami before it began." "Lord, if you had been in Glendale, California, you could have calmed Juan Alvarez's troubled soul and prevented the tragic railroad crash that killed 11 and hurt 180 others." "Lord, if you were here, 200 million people around the globe would not be going hungry tonight." "Lord, if you were in the tomato and berry fields, the workers would not be exploited and robbed of a living wage." "Lord, if you were in Dallas last night, a child would not have been struck with the back of his father's drunken hand." "Lord, if only you had been here . . ."

"Jesus Wept": The Longest Verse in the Bible

My problem is not with Lazarus' resurrection. My problem is with his death. My problem is that so much of my experience ends with John 11:35. I don't get to see verse 39 nearly as often: "*Take away the stone.*" Or verse 43: "*Lazarus, come forth!*" Or verse 44: "*Unbind him, and let him go.*" The stone is still in place, there is no shout into the tomb. The binding is in place. The stench of corpses contaminates the air we try to breathe. I long for the italics, those words that evoke the future, that lean away from the past, from death and *toward* resurrection, but John 11:35 is not in italics. Its letters stand tall, straight, and still.

That's why John 11:35 has become the longest verse in the Bible. Because the gap between John 11:35 and John 11:44 has become so very wide.

Good oral interpreters of Scripture know how to use a pause in order to heighten the aural reception of the text. But if the reader pauses too long, what is there to keep the reader attentive, or even still present?

"Jesus wept."

It took me a long time to realize that this at once very short and very long verse tells us something crucial about God's presence in the world. And that is: we live now at that crossroads where Jesus paused for what seemed like only a brief moment outside of town and entered into the grief of two women and an entire town. That pause has become the essence of our experience of God. It's not what we had in mind, exactly. Yet, it is an ironically hopeful location. His tears and anger are testimony, a confession of faith—faith in a God who is with us in our struggle and pain. A God who does not avoid our grief, but continues—in the presence of the Spirit—to stand with us in a world of loss most of the time as one who still weeps with us, in us, and even through us. The anger and grief we feel when we really engage our lives' and our world's struggles are not the feelings, emotions, and experiences that get in the way of faithful living; they are the stuff of faithful living. It is because we have hoped so much, and believed so much, and risked love so much that we grieve at the edge of town, and that we too are angry at the graveyard. To weep is really to hope. To be angry is really to believe. It is stubborn faith in face of the gospel's embarrassment.[3]

Jesus wept. To weep at loss is to do the work of God in the world. Weeping at loss is not just personal and private work; it is also the public work of protest against the powers of an age that is passing away. To feel what Jesus felt in the face of loss, and also in the face of things that ought not be—that is the indignation that leads to protest. As Shakespeare said at

---

3. Beker, *Paul's Apocalyptic Gospel*, 17.

the end of *King Lear*, "The weight of this sad time we must obey; speak what we feel, not what we ought to say."[4]

God is calling out a new corps of weeping prophets in our day to stand up to the false prophets in politics and religion who preach peace when there is no peace. The weeping, protesting prophets of God are those who give voice to their tears, anger, hope, and expectation through whatever means their mind and body chooses—dance, image, song, gesture, word, graffiti . . . "The words of the prophets are written on the subway walls."[5] The creative catharsis is born of moments when the artist's soul confronts the gap between painful experience and hopeful promise and is truthful to what comes forth as an expression of the ache in between pain and hope.[6]

We are the Jesus that stands on the edge of town now. We are his ambassadors of the resurrection and the life in our bodies and our communities. And as such, we are his weeping presence among those who suffer, lose, and grieve. We are his protesting presence in agitated anticipation of the celebration of resurrection.

We are the resurrection weeping at the edge of hurting cities today. Caught between a gnawing hunger that cramps the spirit and the alluring anticipation of release and freedom, we lean forward—*our spirits italicize*.

Though much of our personal experience attempts to deny or mock the promises, though our lives are at times startlingly tear streaked, though our moral skies are darkened with the soot of hate, violence, and fallible love, streaks of light persistently pierce through the darkness and remind us that the darkness, though ominous, has not overcome the light. Though the fallible love of those in this world has failed us again and again, we have yet experienced real love through these fathers, mothers, brothers, sisters, friends, children, husbands, and wives. Have they ultimately failed to love us as we most needed to be loved, as we yearned to be loved? Yes, many times, yes. Just as we have failed them. But the answer is no, also. Because pure love has gotten, and continues to get, in the mix too. We have been held in an embrace that took us out of time and space and made us aware of something much bigger than ourselves and our losses and our failures. We have known love—love that surprised us, thrilled us, validated us as human beings; love that evoked within us awe, praise, and gratitude. We have seen in the eyes of another the look and gaze of understanding, care,

---

4. Buechner, *Speak What We Feel*, x.
5. Simon and Garfunkel, "The Sound of Silence" (Columbia Studios, 1964).
6. Resner, "Social Justice," 135–37.

and ultimate concern. Looking into those eyes that locked on us, we were granted a portal to the Divine gaze, the Divine love, the Divine promises. We need a community of nurture, where this love is allowed to breathe.

When Lazarus was sick and Mary and Martha could do nothing to help him, they did the only thing they knew to do: they sent for Jesus, and they waited. But we, as Mary and Martha today waiting on Jesus to come, wait not passively. We wait together, forming communities of active protestation against every action, every word, every law, every political and economic decision that hurts any human being. In the wake of continued human suffering, we continue to send for the deliverance that only God can bring, and in the meantime we protest the violence by our presence with those who suffer, by our tears on their behalf and ours, by our outcry to God, by our internal groaning for the more that we have been promised, in the sighing that the Spirit turns into sane and articulate prayer before God (Rom 8:14–27).

Amen.

3

Getting Our Hopes Screwed on Straight: Navigating Our Emmaus Road

(Meditation, Reflection, and Proclamation on Luke 24:13–35)

"What's this you're discussing so intently as you walk along?" Then one of them, his name was Cleopas, said, "Are you the only one in Jerusalem who hasn't heard what's happened during the last few days?" He said, "What has happened?" They said, "The things that happened to Jesus the Nazarene, He was a man of God, a prophet, dynamic in work and word, blessed by both God and all the people. Then our high priests and leaders betrayed him, got him sentenced to death, and crucified him. *And we had our hopes up that he was the one*, the one about to deliver Israel . . ." (Luke 24:17–21a, *The Message*, emphasis added)

TRUTH BE TOLD, I think everyone plays the game "If I Were God" from time to time. It goes something like this: "If I were God, I would not allow war in this world. If I were God, no one would go to bed hungry, angry, hopeless, or feeling unloved. If I were God, everyone would have a bed and a home and three square meals a day. If I were God gasoline would be twenty-five cents a gallon and there would be no credit card or student loan debt. Work weeks would be Tuesday through Thursday and weekends would be Friday through Monday. Everyone would be in jobs that were fulfilling and overpaid. At home, nothing would break, decay, or get dirty. The grass would grow an inch high and stop, and the yard would never need watering or weeding. O yeah, and there would be no mosquitos. If I were God, there would be no back or neck pain and exercise would be fun. Sleep would be at least eight hours every night, without interruptions—no night sweats, insomnia, anxious thoughts, worries about children, retirement, job security, or personal safety."

Now, with that platform, if we lived in a democratic cosmos, wouldn't you vote for me to be God? I suspect the two hundred million people who went to sleep hungry last night, many without beds or homes, might think I'd make a better God than the one who allowed their hunger to continue.

There is something that the game of "If I Were God" reveals: it shows us what we really want from God. And if I'm honest, what I want from God reveals in me a mixture. It reveals a mixture of thoughtfulness for others on the one hand, but on the other hand, some good old-fashioned self-centered greed. If I could dictate God's actions, I'd want others, especially those who suffer, to be taken care of, but I'd make sure that I was happy, healthy, wealthy, and wise, and that those I cared about were too. There can't be too much wrong with that, can there? It's sort of like when we remind God that we'd be exactly the right persons to win the lottery for all the philanthropic good we'd do (along with a new car and vacation to Maui).

But here's the problem, as I pry the lid off my motives for wanting to be God: it is my perceived needs and problems that set the agenda for the God I want. What makes that a problem? The problem is that, because I think I'm so right about the way things ought to be, I start expecting the real God, the God who is separate from my own cognitive projections and fantasies, to act in alignment with my perceptions of reality. And when God doesn't act accordingly, and in ways that fit my perceived needs, then I become like those two disciples on the road to Emmaus, with hopes and dreams dashed. And it gets even worse.

Often my expectations of God often become so powerful, since I, of course, in all my wisdom, know so well how God ought to act, that those expectations keep my eyes blind to what God has really promised, and blind to the ways that God is actually at work in this world—ways that I do not recognize because my interests, desires, and expectations, are elsewhere.

Have you ever let yourself get your hopes up for how God might act only to have those hopes dashed? I have to make a hard confession that I would rather not make, especially as an ordained minister. I find it very hard sometimes to pray for people who are sick to get well. I want to pray for their healing, and I do end up doing so, but at the same time, I find myself afraid to invest myself in the hope that they might actually be cured.

In 1972, when I had just earned my driver's permit at age fifteen, my dad and I drove tag-team straight through the night from Carlsbad, California, to Temple, Texas, to be with my grandmother, Bubba, who was dying of cancer. When we arrived, I remember hardly even recognizing her in the hospital bed. She had lost so much weight and was so weak. Everyone was speaking in hushed tones around her. It seemed that all involved—family, friends, doctors, and nurses—had resigned themselves to the fact that she would die, and hopefully soon. I was appalled by their collective lack of faith. These were, after all, supposedly church folk, Bible-believing Christians. How could they so easily give up? When we would go back to her house where we stayed during that time, I would pray as I never had prayed before, with boldness and confidence, just as Jesus had said to do. I said, "This is our chance, God, to prove to everyone that your power is greater than death. We can show them that you can overcome anything in this world, even cancer. *Raise her from that bed, God! Raise her!*" Like the Bible said, I asked it in faith and I believed that I had received my answer in advance. I returned to the hospital day after day confident and expectant, fully believing that God would raise her up and amaze everyone. I couldn't wait to stand up in the worshipping assembly, with my grandmother next to me, and exclaim to all present, just like the psalmist, that God had brought her back from the brink of death to the land of the living.

At her funeral I felt like someone had scooped out my insides and left nothing but a hollow space. I did not pray for a long time after the drive back from Texas to California. I held back in instances that I knew I should be praying, but I couldn't allow myself to get my hopes up. Then, in two subsequent incidents, at the hospital beds of people that I could not imagine my life without, I tried to pray again in 100 percent trust and anticipation that God would work the miracle that I wanted, that I needed, but both those people died too. And when they did, a lot of my hopes and dreams died with them.

I have known disappointment with God. And just like the disciples on the Emmaus road who had the hope knocked out of them, I had Bible verses to support my hopes. You see, those disciples hadn't just fabricated hopes for the Messiah on their own. They read their Bibles and their eyes were attracted to the verses that supported their hopes. They had texts where God promised to always have a king on the throne, a son of David. They had texts where God promised to always protect Jerusalem, the now Roman-occupied city, which in Luke's day was bereft even of the temple, looted and leveled by Rome's military leader, Titus. They had stories of God leading them triumphantly through bloody battles, clearing the promised land for them to occupy, and destroying all rival kings and kingdoms in their path, thus establishing them as the most enviable nation on earth. In the same way, I could see lots of places throughout the Bible, and especially in the Gospels, where God restored the health of the near-dead, and even the dead-dead.

Of course, another person can find Bible verses to support his desire to become really wealthy—*ahem*, I mean "blessed." Another can find verses to support having lots of real estate—*ahem*, "expanded borders." And another can find verses that promise her health, thinness, beauty, fame, safety, even the blessedness of a nice tan. Thus we all have our scissor-and-paste wish list, and we pray, and we think positively and we smile a lot and are nice to the elderly and puppies, and we fully expect that all of this positive spiritual energy will auto-magically generate "our best lives now"—Christian karma as it were. Whatever the perceived need, there will always be verses to justify our desire and verses to construct the God who will give us what we want.

All of this sounds a little suspect, even selfish, greedy, and idolatrous. Is the proper procedure in understanding the gospel to start with *our* perceived needs and *our* perceived desires? Or, does the gospel itself set the agenda and help orient us to what our real needs are? For instance, did the gospel ever promise us that those we love would not die? Not really; in fact, the New Testament's bold claim is that the gospel promises us resurrection, not death prevention. Did we forget that the unfortunate prerequisite for resurrection is death?

When did the gospel promise us perpetual financial success? The gospel, in fact, warns us that if we put our trust in riches, that misplaced trust will threaten our ability to enter the Kingdom of God. When did the gospel promise that if we are good Americans then God will not allow anyone to penetrate our borders with violence, terror, and death? The gospel instead warns us that no earthly kingdom or government is divine or inviolable. No matter how much we have personally invested in an earthly citizenship, the gospel thwarts our patriotism when it reminds us that our true citizenship is in heaven. The gospel urges us to put our ultimate trust in a government that is not of this world: the Kingdom of God, one that will never be ultimately defeated by any power of evil or darkness. When did the gospel ever promise that we will not feel pain, sickness, or chronic physical difficulties? The gospel promises instead that even though we may have "thorns in the flesh" that will not go away even with repeated prayer, God's grace is nevertheless sufficient for us. When were we ever promised that the Holy Spirit will always keep us warm, comfy, and happy? The gospel promised instead that the Spirit would abide with us in our suffering, helping us to cry out to God, groan in our pain, and offer prayer through our sighs of despair. It is that accompanying Spirit of God who will interpret to God the yearnings of our hearts when we cannot find words to describe how we feel or to name what we need.

Getting one's hope up for something, only to have it dashed, can leave one stuck. As a child, I let myself get my hopes up for answered prayer to cure my grandmother of cancer. She died. Something broke within me. Those disciples Jesus encountered on the Emmaus road let themselves dream big and bet heavy on Jesus. Then he was killed. Something broke inside of them.

I guess you cannot blame us for doing so, but the truth is that we keep hoping for things from the gospel that the gospel never promised. And when God doesn't show up and deliver what we want, when we want it, we chuck our faith, we chuck our God, or we blame our lack of faith and piety, or consider ourselves unworthy of God's attention because of some sin that disqualifies us from God's care. In any case, failure to get what we want, when we want it, the way we want it leads to a familiar conclusion: we just quit getting our hopes up for fear that we'll just be disappointed again.

"*And we had our hopes up that he was the one*, the one about to deliver Israel . . ." That's our point of contact with this story at the end of Luke's Gospel. They had gotten their hopes up that "*he* was the one," that "he would *deliver*." The New Revised Standard Version translates it: "*But we had hoped that he was the one to redeem Israel.*" Another good translation for the word "deliver" would be "free." Because those first disciples on the Emmaus road, dragging their feet and their hearts along the desolate road, were just having it sink in that their hopes for deliverance and freedom from the long oppression of the Roman occupation would not end any time soon. And their hopes that God was decisively showing up in the new king, the long-overdue Messiah, were now decisively shattered since Roman officials had murdered Jesus, and as if to put an exclamation point onto his failed kingship, they did so in the most humiliating manner possible—by crucifixion. It drove home poignantly how stupid they had been to get their hopes up for some miraculous, divine intervention into their situation of suffering and despair. In fact, because they had allowed themselves to hope again, and so extravagantly, they had sunken even deeper into the hole of despondency. You can almost hear their thoughts: "*And we will never let that happen again."* Jesus' death meant the death of their hopes for a different future.

But Luke's story also shows that their hopes in what God would do, and how God would deliver, were misplaced. Their hopes were idolatrous and self-serving. They wouldn't have, and maybe couldn't have, seen it that way, of course. Their motives could have been seen to be pure, and even biblically driven. But the fuller revelation of resurrection, of course, turns the tables over on all our best guesses, hopes, and expectations for how God ought to act on our behalf. The resurrection opens our eyes to our self-deceptions and unending pursuit of self-serving "gospels" of our own making.

That exposure of misplaced hope is part of the good news of this story. Because in spite of their false hopes, God still comes among them, mysteriously and hidden, and even somewhat mischievously, since Jesus acts like he has no clue what is going on. He seems to be having a little too much fun with his resurrection, playing dumb and leading them on. In fact, however, he leads them down a path that results in their own confession of misplaced hope.

The Emmaus revelation shows us a God who continues to come among us to unmask our idolatries and self-serving hopes and expectations and at the same time unveils God's and our true destiny. And here in Luke 24 God does that through the means of word and sacrament, both hidden signs of surprising disclosure when we least expect it. God is faithful still.

In face of the struggles that Luke's own community of faith was having in the aftermath of the temple's defilement and subsequent destruction in 70 CE and later, Luke points to two familiar places in his church's experience to try to reframe their hopes and dreams. He used the Emmaus story to say to his church, "Jesus is still among us even when we are blind to his presence. He still comes among us in the word and at the table, even when we do not see him. Even when we do not understand. Even when we have put unfair expectations on God and are blinded by our own misplaced hopes and the attendant grief of their unfulfillment. Even when we're just going through the motions of church, of family, work, or life. All of these things can 'keep our eyes from recognizing him,' but Jesus is still present with disciples whose hopes feel like they've been beat to death by disappointment."

To get at the gospel that this story relates, look at what the hidden Jesus does. He sees them. He comes to them and he teases out of them their disappointments. As we noted already, the beginning of Luke's Emmaus story borders on the absurd, or the hilarious, when we realize that the Jesus who had just been arrested, mocked, beaten, scourged, crucified, and buried could join up with a couple of guys seven miles from Jerusalem, of all places, and innocently ask, "So, what are you guys talking about?" And after they exasperatedly ask, "Are you the only human being who doesn't know the things that have happened in the last few days?" Jesus, the only one who actually does know what's really taken place, asks, "What things?" He sure is in a better mood on Easter than he was on Good Friday! But notice what he does next with these two men on the Emmaus road.

He teases out their disappointments. He confronts their false hopes. He opens their eyes by a fresh interpretation of the Scriptures. He shakes them out of the ruts of their reading of the Scriptures, ruts that only rendered to them what they wanted to see, what they were predisposed to see. And in their new hearing, their hearts burn within them as Jesus opens up the Scriptures to them.

I can imagine Luke's community having an "aha" moment when they realized that that's what was actually going on every week when they gathered for worship, read Scripture, and listened for God's word: "He is still among us!"

I grew up in a small town in Texas, north of Austin. I lived in town but my cousin lived on a nearly seven-hundred-acre ranch outside of town. As young boys in the early 60s, we would roam the ranch together imagining we were real cowboys and ranch hands. But before we were let loose out there alone with our jeans, boots, hats, and BB guns, my uncle gave us a stern talking to. After telling us not to shoot anything that was alive—especially the cows—and to watch out for rattlesnakes, copperheads, red ants, and scorpions, he said, "Boys, on a ranch you've got to get, and keep, your heads screwed on straight or lots of bad things can happen to you out there." He really scared us. He meant to. And his point was crystal clear: to survive in the wild you have to keep your wits about you; in other words, get, and keep, your head screwed on straight. Survival is possible, and it can even be adventurous, but you can never forget while out there to keep your mental bearings sober and alert.

Jesus' confrontation with the disappointed disciples on the Emmaus road, his re-teaching of Scripture to them, and his graceful and revealing presence with them in the breaking of the bread were all efforts to help those hopeless disciples get their hopes screwed back on straight. For disciples of Jesus many, many centuries later, living under quite different skies and with quite different concerns, our question persists: in what ways does this text tell us about how God might still be with us?

Luke set Jesus' appearance with the disciples on the Emmaus squarely in the context of the breaking of bread at the table. That was not an accident. It was Luke's way of telling his community sometime after 70 CE that Jesus was still gracefully, mercifully, and reorientingly present in the sacrament that they were participating in. He wanted all communities that came after his to realize the same revelatory possibility in both word and sacrament: Jesus is present here. Jesus opens our eyes here. Jesus opens the Scriptures here and our hearts burn afresh.

Yet, at the same time, Jesus cannot be imprisoned here. Just as he gracefully and freely shows up in our ignorance to reveal himself, Luke tells us that the moment of revelation is accompanied by a simultaneous moment of elusiveness: "Then their eyes were opened, and they recognized him; *and he vanished from their sight*" (24:31). It is a bizarre twist in the plot. I would expect the characters in that moment to exclaim, "Where did he go?!?! He was just here. You saw him too, right?" But Luke seems to think Jesus' bizarre disappearance is normal. Their moment of revelation flashed before their eyes and consciousness. But before they could bottle it up, the moment and Jesus were mysteriously gone.

Unfazed by this crazy sequence of events, Luke says that the two men immediately reflected on how their hearts burned within them when they recalled Jesus opening up the Scriptures to them on the road, and then they bounded the eight miles back to Jerusalem to tell everyone that Jesus had risen. Clearly, this is a resurrection appearance, and thus a resurrection confirmation story. But more than that it makes a powerful theological claim about the revelatory efficacy of both the Word and the sacrament at the same time that it cautions the humans who are involved in the administration and stewardship of the Word and the sacraments that they are not in charge, or in control, of the word's or the table's revelatory efficacy—only God is. For just when the humans involved think they've got it, think they see it, it escapes their sight and grasp. God's self-disclosure eludes human attempts to freeze-frame it, and even manipulate it or reproduce it for the masses. Luke is saying that God remains free in God's revelation, even elusive and hidden. That means that humans cannot franchise revelation, put it on a clock, or even program it liturgically.

When God shows up it is a gift, always a free, undeserved, unpredictable, and unprogrammable gift. That does not mean that we do not set assembly times for worship, and do all we can to set the stage through worship and preaching to hear a word and to see God present. We do all that, and pray that we might be given eyes to see what God has to show us, and ears to listen so that we might hear what God has to say to us. It is to say that no matter what we do, or how we do it, we cannot constrain God's revelation by our efforts. God remains free.

Jesus' elusive and sudden departure does not change, however, what happened to these formerly hope-shattered disciples. They were now hope filled as they realized that Jesus, though crucified, was not defeated. Jesus, though killed, was no longer dead. Now was the time for them to glorify God in face of this surprising turn of events, but also to re-evaluate hope based on this new fact. And that is true for us as well, we who are disciples these many centuries later. For God's reversal of Jesus' death in the miracle of resurrection means that death and loss, grieve and suffering, do not get the final word in this world. This does not of course do away with our grief and loss, but it does put our grief and loss within a frame of perspective. As Paul said to the churches in Thessalonica, we do not "grieve as others who have no hope" (1 Thess 4:13). Put in the positive, Christians grieve, yes, but as those with hope. In other words, our grief is not a bottomless pit of despair. There is a bottom to it. There is an end to it. It will not and cannot consume us forever, because all the death, loss, and grief that the world knows is now shown to be a temporary condition in light of the revelation of the resurrection of Jesus. His resurrection is the first of many. His triggers the end of the old age and the beginning of the New. His resurrection is so momentous that Paul can even characterize the deaths of those who have been water-buried and raised in Christ as a mere sleep from which they shall wake when Jesus comes again. This is our Hope (note, with a capital H) now and it changes everything. Because disciples can now live courageously in the world, confident that God's ultimate outcome has already been assured in Jesus' defeat of death and death's power.

Perhaps no New Testament writer captures hope's new vision better than the apostle John, who, exiled on the island of Patmos, saw through the eye of faith this image of God's coming city:

> Then I saw a new heaven and a new earth, for the first heaven and the first earth had passed away. And I saw the holy city, the new Jerusalem, coming down out of heaven from God, prepared as a bride adorned for her husband. And I heard a loud voice from the throne saying, "See, the home of God is among mortals. He will

dwell with them as their God. They will be his peoples, and God himself will be with them; he will wipe every tear from their eyes. Death will be no more; mourning and crying and pain will be no more, for the first things have passed away." And the one who was seated on the throne said, "See, I am making all things new." Also he said, "Write this, for these words are trustworthy and true." Then he said to me, "It is done! I am the Alpha and the Omega, the beginning and the end. To the thirsty I will give water as a gift from the spring of the water of life." (Rev 21:1–6)

That is a Hope to screw on straight, and to keep on straight, in this world of continuing and ever new deceptions.

4

Breathing Prayer: Learning the Language of the Spirit

(Meditation, Reflection, and Proclamation on Romans 8:12–27)

AFTER GUEST-PREACHING A SERIES of four sermons on Mark's Gospel at a church in New Jersey, a woman thirty years my senior came to me and asked if she could come to my office for a chat. That Tuesday, Jean came by mid-morning. She asked me if I would be her spiritual adviser.

Jean had been an elder in the church for decades. Her husband, now retired, had been a pastor for over fifty years. I was a little perplexed by her request and frankly felt overwhelmed and inadequate by it. But she insisted. It was the kind of insistence that I've learned to listen to. I told her that she was going to have to help me know how she thought I could help her.

She wasted no time. She told me of a painful experience she had as a little girl. It had plagued her for her entire life. It had rendered her unable to pray. She couldn't throw away her conviction that there was a God, but she didn't know how to relate to a God who had not protected her when she needed it. In spite of her relentless anguish, and inability to pray, for years Jean had been a leader, perhaps even the most significant leader, at the church for which I had been guest-preaching. Many looked to her as a sage, spiritual guide, and shepherd. The fact that I was not part of that circle made me a safe place for her to tell her difficult truths. As we began these meetings, though, I still wasn't clear who was spiritually directing whom.

All I could do during our first meeting was listen to her story. She spoke calmly yet with measured intensity. I took in her words, but I had no words in return. I felt like a failure.

Later that week I was listening to Dave Matthews' song "Grey Street," and I thought of Jean. It's a ballad about a woman who "goes stumbling

Breathing Prayer: Learning the Language of the Spirit

through her memories," wondering, "How did I come to this?" Her dilemma is poignant.

> There's an emptiness inside her
> and she'd do anything to fill it in
> but all the colors mix together—to grey
> and it breaks her heart
>
> How she wishes it was different
> She prays to God most every night
> and though she swears it doesn't listen
> there's a tiny hope in her it might
>
> She says, "I pray"
> but they fall on deaf ears,
> Am I supposed to take it on myself
> to get out of this place?

When Jean came back the next week I played her the song. When it ended, she said, "That's me." She took the CD with her and next week said, "I listened to the song dozens of times this week. I resonated so deeply . . . except for one thing: I can't pray. I try. But there are no words." I told her that when we cannot ourselves pray, we can lean on the community around us to intercede for us. But even as I trotted out this hoped-for solution to her prayer problem, hearing myself say it, I felt like an idiot. Maybe I was technically true and right in what I said to her, but it felt hollow and trite when I saw what I said reflected back in her pleading eyes.

After my platitudes, I then ventured out onto, for me, previously unchartered ground. I told her that hearing her story had forced me to go back to the New Testament, scouring its pages with her and her words in my ears. Eventually, I found myself in Romans 8. I was startled by what I saw. Paul's words stopped me in my tracks and I read them over and over. But it wasn't the part of Romans 8 that people often quote, namely, the cross-stitchable, triumphant words of Romans 8:28: "We know that all things work together for good for those who love God, who are called according to his purpose." That is the well-worn panacea verse, the cure-all for every ill, the smiley-faced band-aid stuck on everything from a scratch to cancer. It was also spiritually dismissive of those whose pain and anguish wouldn't be, perhaps couldn't be, taken seriously.

No, the section that spoke to me as the bearer of Jean's pain was the section that preceded verse 28, where Paul develops his understanding of the role of the Holy Spirit in the life of God's in-between-time people. How are God's creatures to survive in a world of suffering, decay, and death while they attempt to maintain hope that what God has started in Jesus' death and resurrection will ultimately be completed?

Paul envisions a New Humanity in much the same predicament that Jean found herself in. He paints the portrait of a humanity that, on the one hand, is a victim of this world's continued violence and terror, and that, on the other hand, is a victor in the wake of God's call and claim on her life in the gospel, a call and claim made tangible and palpable in her baptism. This New Humanity feels painfully its participation in a world that is passing away, while at the same time struggles to embrace the truth of the New Day that is dawning. This new humanity has one foot in the old age and one foot in the New.

I read Paul's words to Jean from Romans 8. She understood the concepts, and wanted it all to be true, but she told me that if she was honest with herself, she could not feel the New Dawning Day to the same extent as the one that was passing away into the darkness. The ache of being stuck, even drowning, in the old world eclipsed any relief that the other foot, stretching forward into the New Age, might have sensed.

I turned again to Romans 8:14–27 and asked her to listen again as I read.

> For all who are led by the Spirit of God are children of God. For you did not receive a spirit of slavery to fall back into fear, but you have received a spirit of adoption. *When we cry, "Abba! Father!" it is that very Spirit bearing witness with our spirit that we are children of God*, and if children, then heirs, heirs of God and joint heirs with Christ—if, in fact, we suffer with him so that we may also be glorified with him. I consider that the sufferings of this present time are not worth comparing with the glory about to be revealed to us. For the creation waits with eager longing for the revealing of the children of God; for the creation was subjected to futility, not of its own will but by the will of the one who subjected it, in hope that the creation itself will be set free from its bondage to decay and will obtain the freedom of the glory of the children of God. We know that the whole creation has been groaning in labor pains until now; and not only the creation, *but we ourselves, who have the first fruits of the Spirit, groan inwardly while we wait for adoption, the redemption of our bodies.* For in hope we were saved. Now hope that is seen is not hope. For who hopes for what is seen? But if we hope for what we do not see, we wait for it with

> patience. Likewise the Spirit helps us in our weakness; *for we do not know how to pray as we ought, but that very Spirit intercedes with sighs too deep for words.* And God, who searches the heart, knows what is the mind of the Spirit, because the Spirit intercedes for the saints according to the will of God.

I have italicized the three places where Paul indicates a kind of co-operation between the Holy Spirit and our human spirits in face of humanity's in-between-time status. The Spirit leads us, makes us children of God, and gives us a spirit of adoption. Our *cries* to God, "*Abba! Father!*," are evidence that God's Spirit and ours both bear witness to these truths. There is also a solidarity—a shared epistemology (way of knowing or understanding) and ontology (way of existing or being), if you will—between the created order and us, and that solidarity expresses itself in *groans*. Those groans are the articulation of the painful gap between the initiation of our adoption and the fulfillment of that adoption. Those testifying groans are like the sound of tectonic plates grinding together underground at a fault line during an earthquake. Paul asserts that what God has begun in the death and resurrection of Jesus is to shift the plates at the underground fault line of history, a shifting that signals the end of the old and beginning of the New.

Creation itself, Paul says, knows what we feel, and groans as well. The metaphor Paul uses for creation's painful, as yet unfulfilled experience is similar to that of "adoption," the metaphor he uses for the New Humanity. Paul says that creation is suffering in the midst of the throes of labor. Both adoption and labor pains symbolize the emergence of new life, the hope of enlarged family relations, but both metaphors also convey the incompleteness, pain, and often exhausting anticipation of an imminent completion and fulfillment.

An orphan who has been given the good news that she has been chosen to be part of a new family is gleeful as she prepares to meet her new parents and family, and eventually go home, but she also anxiously desires that the consummation of the adoption take place. After being told that she has been adopted, after she finishes packing, she is eager to get this new life started. If she sits in the waiting room of the orphanage too long, surrounded by her luggage, excitement turns to frustration, even anguish and doubt. How long can she continue to tell others of her good fortune, her future life, before she and all others begin to wonder if it is really true, or merely wishful thinking?

PART 1—MEDITATIONS AND REFLECTIONS

The woman who is nine months pregnant whose water breaks, and who begins to feel the wave of contractions, struggles in the throes of labor. She attempts to strike a balance between the rhythmic pain of the process and the joyful anticipation of new life. Yet unless she is anesthetized, the pain threshold usually overwhelms the sense of outcome. The breathing strategies and focal-point exercises are attempts to manage the process to completion, if not distract from the pain, struggle, and feeling of loss of control.

The longer each person waits and endures, from the moment the adoption or the labor begins, the more difficult each hour becomes. An extended waiting period also allows fear and doubt to creep into consciousness, with the thought that maybe I was a fool for believing that this might go well, much less end as I had hoped.

Paul indicates that the waiters—the orphan/adoptee, the pregnant woman/new mother—begin to engage in a new kind of language during the delay, namely that of *crying, groaning, and sighing*. Each utterance is unrehearsed, guttural, impromptu, without self-consciousness or self-editing. Yet they are the utterances of truth in the face of adversity. At the end of one's capacity to endure, one cries out. When the suffering becomes intolerable, one involuntary groans. When exasperation overwhelms, one sighs. This is the linguistic trinity that rises out of despair. In face of this turmoil, Paul makes the bold, if not outright incredible, claim that for the New Humanity who aches for God's Kingdom to fully come, these utterances—the cries, groans, and sighs—are evidence that the Spirit is at work in and through them.

I asked Jean, "Do you ever find yourself crying, groaning, or sighing uncontrollably?" She replied weakly, "All the time." I said, "Does it make a difference for you to hear that those cries, groans, and sighs are not the utterances of failure and despair, but rather evidence that God's Spirit is with you, in you, co-operating with your spirit to keep you connected to God, God's promises, and that in these involuntary utterances you can take refuge, solace, and even comfort that God hasn't given up on you—is even using those actions and sounds to pray through you?" "Yes, I think it does," she said.

I asked, "May we try an exercise?" "Sure." "I'd like you to close your eyes and just breathe. Take in a slow, deep, measured breath, and then let it all the way out. Try to completely fill your lungs, then totally release every bit of breath. Keep doing this, one after another. Don't go too quickly, though; I don't want you to hyperventilate."

As she began the breathing sequence, I then began to talk to her, trying to orient her to a different understanding, experience, and practice, of prayer.

"In the very beginning of creation, when everything was still a formless void and darkness covered the face of the deep, the *ruach* of God—God's Spirit, breath, wind—swept over the face of the waters. In the middle of the chaos, God's Spirit brooded; God's Spirit was present. Then God's voice, God's word, began to bring order to the chaos. God said, 'Let there be light!' And there was light.

"Spirit, Word, Light, over against the formless void, the deep, the darkness. And which prevailed? Which relented?" Jean continued her slow, measured, deep breathing. I let time pass.

"In the second creation account, we are told that God formed the human from the dust of the ground and animated him as a living being by breathing into his nostrils the breath of life. It is God's breath that makes the human being live. If we stop breathing for even five or ten minutes, we experience brain damage. After fifteen minutes, we will most likely die.

"Did God rig our most basic, needed element for living—oxygen—to remind us that we cannot live without God, without God's *pneuma*, *ruach*, the Breath and Spirit of God for even a few minutes? We fast from food as a spiritual discipline. It reminds us that just as we need food to remain alive, if we are without God we die a greater death. But we cannot fast from breathing. It is too elemental to our existence. And yet we breathe unconsciously. Unless we are ill, or unusually self-conscious, we go through our every day breathing in and out, not cognizant of our ever-precarious situation—if we stop breathing, we die." Again I paused.

"If Paul is right that the gift to us of the Spirit/Breath of God helps us to articulate the truth of our ache between the times, then the truest prayer may be nothing more than breathing, than crying, than groaning and sighing. Breathing from the deepest place within ourselves. Breathing in God's animating life and exhaling. Could this be what Paul means about 'praying without ceasing?'" Again I paused for a couple of minutes while she breathed slowly in and out.

"Jean, with each inhale, I want you to imagine that you are taking in God's life-animating breath. With each exhale, imagine that you are releasing the spirit-sapping toxins of disappointment[1] . . . defeat . . . frustration . . . longing . . . despair . . . violence . . . pain. [Long pause] With each inhale, imagine that you are taking into your lungs the spirit-enlivening nutrients of hope[2] . . . victory . . . fulfillment . . . joy. As you take in these words of promise, feel them penetrate the walls of your lungs and enter into your bloodstream. Feel them travel to all regions of your being, saturating your entire self with God's recreating word of Shalom. Exhale the past: the old, broken creation that is passing away, the one that God has begun to put an end to with the crucifixion of Jesus. Inhale the New Creation that God has inaugurated with Jesus' resurrection. And trust that with every exhale, every cry, groan, and sigh that you emit this week the Spirit of God is partnering with your spirit to bring before the almighty God the wordless prayers from the deepest place of your ache. Whenever you catch yourself engaged in these extemporaneous actions and utterances, remember that they are the work of God's Spirit in conjunction with your own. Know that God is filling in the blanks of the prayers that you do not have words for. Know that not having words to pray is not failure on your part; rather, it is a tacit knowing that there are no words anywhere within the old creation for expressing the ache and longing of living between the times. [Pause] Embrace God's Spirit moving in and through you when feel every cry, groan, and sigh, and when these things happen embrace them as the 'first fruits,' the 'guarantee,' and the 'down payment' on God's New Creation that these moves of the Spirit within you are. Until he comes.

"Go ahead and open your eyes whenever you're ready. How do you feel, Jean?" "Different." "Different good, I hope." "Yes, different good, especially compared to how I came in here today."

Reflection and Interpretation

I met with Jean for about a year before a job transition took me to another state. What we had begun in those sessions continued, with the practice of breathing prayer becoming an integral aspect of her new spiritual practice. It also became part of my own.

My experience with Jean brought several things together for me that had been brewing in my own faith struggle for many years: grief, lament, the ache and yearning for justice and rectification, the promise of the gospel,

---

1. I waited to say each one of these words with each of her exhalations.
2. Again, I waited to say of these words with each of her inhalations.

the odd predicament of living between the times, theodicy (the questions about the love and justice of God in a suffering world), and solidarity with an aching and yearning creation. I often wondered what drew Jean to me after hearing me preach those four sermons on Mark. My guess is that she sensed something behind those sermons, in me the preacher, something that I have come to call mournfulness. Mark's message and Mark's Jesus are dark and brooding in my reading of his Gospel. There is a realism that pulses in his story, a realism that refigures how we are to understand the gospel as good news. We must, of course, bracket out the chorus of voices coming from Matthew, Luke, and John, for Mark sings in a minor key and does not harmonize with their more cheery trio. For all the similarities among the so-called Synoptic Gospels—Matthew, Mark, and Luke—Mark remains the most unlike the others, including John, not because of content or chronology or theology, but because of tenor, tone, and broodiness.

Grief is the human experience and emotion that follows loss. It is the ache one feels in place of the person or thing that now is gone. Much of human existence consists in negotiating the terrain of grief. Many have rightly described the processes of grief as somewhat chartable and predictable, yet also unique in the details of each individual and loss. When I attempted to access my earliest experiences of grief, I kept coming back to the experience of finding the partial remains of my pet rabbit in my backyard. It had been ravaged by our dog. I had always disliked that dog. Now I hated it. I remember sitting on my mother's lap in the kitchen of our Texas home, weeping what seemed like endless tears. She just held me and rocked me back and forth, like the gentle cycle of a washing machine, slowly rinsing from my spirit the pain I felt. Eventually the tears stopped. Some part of the ache still exists, compounded by the years of ensuing losses and subsequent experiences of grief.

Nothing in my experience of loss and grief compared to the death of my son in December of 1986. The world ground to a halt for me. I was almost half way through my MDiv degree program and did not care at that point whether I finished or not. I felt finished already—with life. Every night I would go to bed praying that I would not wake in the morning. Every morning I would awake to the realization that it was true all over again. He was dead. I would never see him again. Hear him again. Hold him again. His future, previously so alive in my own imagination, was gone. I could not imagine my own future without him. When the realization hit me afresh each morning, I would begin shaking uncontrollably for ten to twenty minutes. I couldn't understand why I kept waking up every morning when he had failed to.

There were several people who kept me in school at that time. One was my Old Testament professor, Jim Roberts. One Friday afternoon I was on my way to the administration building of the seminary to withdraw from the school. I thought I should tell Jim first since he had been so instrumental in my life and studies up to that point. He also had adopted me as a son, and my son as his grandson. Jim knew what it was like to lose an only son, having lost his Nathaniel at age six. I went to his back door, knocked, and after he answered to door, told him that I was leaving. He told me to hold on, grabbed two beers from his refrigerator, and asked me to join him on the porch. We sat and sipped on our beers. I don't remember anything we said to each other. What I do remember is that he kept me there until the offices were closed for the weekend. When I realized what he had done, I was a bit miffed, but also bemused by his crafty deception. I do remember what he then said: "Go to school on Monday as if you are in school. And do the same thing on Tuesday, Wednesday, and the rest of the week." I did. It was forced motion. I didn't want to be doing this anymore. I couldn't see the point. My insides had been scooped out. Faith was gone. Why study theology, prepare for ministry, or do exegesis of the Bible when nothing made sense any longer?

What happened to me over those months and years to follow was an intensification of my own examination of everything pertaining to faith and its claims. I had no patience for trite explanations or assertions. My already quite accurate B.S. meter was now at maximum strength. I don't think I was the nicest person to be around most of the time. Hermeneutically, I experienced a revolution. I continued to read the Bible; indeed, the quest to "search the Scriptures" had taken on a quite new intensity. My experience of loss and grief, coupled with a persistent questioning of all the old answers, caused old texts to which I had formerly been blind and deaf to almost glow as I read them. They would find me, those texts, in surprising contexts.

All who have anything to do with faith, and who inform their faith by some connection with the Bible, have two key operatives, whether they are conscious of them or not. One is a sense of Scripture's theological center or core, what I call a "working gospel," and the other is a hermeneutic, i.e., a way of interpreting and applying Scripture's message to one's life and one's world. One's working core serves one's hermeneutic, and helps to sort

Breathing Prayer: Learning the Language of the Spirit

readings and interpretations, especially for the purposes of preaching. The two—working gospel/core and hermeneutic—are intimately related.

The first, one's sense of Scripture's center, has sometimes been called a person's "canon within the canon." This, I believe is too rigid a designation. I concur with David Tracy, who labeled the interpreter's sense of center as a "working canon." "Each theologian has, in fact, some 'working canon' for both the situation and the message to serve as an ordering principle for all theology, including christology [sic]."[3] The idea of a working canon suggests fluidity and adaptation to continued reflection.

Nevertheless, for most interpreters, some texts function more significantly as expressing the heart of the matter more than others. For me, the theological themes that resound through Romans 8:14–27 increasingly serve as the lens through which I understand profound implications of the gospel for sustaining faith, especially as people of faith attempt to make sense of life in the Spirit in the intermediary period between Jesus' appearances. That text's themes thus also become the lens through which I read other texts with a view to preaching the gospel. It therefore informs my hermeneutic (my approach to interpretation) and my homiletic (my approach to what ought to be preached in the texts).

To acknowledge one's own sense of center/working gospel and hermeneutic is important. To be in denial about it is dangerous. As Hans Georg Gadamer warned in direct reference to historicists who, self-deceivingly, liked to claim hermeneutical objectivity, "It is the tyranny of hidden prejudices that makes us deaf to what speaks to us in tradition."[4] For Gadamer, a prejudice was not considered to be a clouding negative as one came to the biblical text. Rather, a prejudice was a necessary hermeneutical presupposition that all interpreters came to the Scriptures with, whether they acknowledged such or not. Gadamer especially had historicists in mind who claimed too much for the efficacy of fastidiously applied methodology in rendering objectively pure interpretations of texts. Ironically, for those historicists, their overestimation of the power of methodology, rightly wielded, to guarantee right interpretation elevated methodology above the text. Historical methodology actually became the authority, not the biblical text. But such a position was actually a ruse, a mirage, a self-deception, and, theologically speaking, a modernist venture into idolatry. Gadamer wanted interpreters to "come clean" with their presuppositions so that they could

---

3. Tracy, *Analogical Imagination*, 254.
4. Gadamer, *Truth and Method*, 270.

honestly grapple with them in conversation with the tradition, including Scripture. The "what speaks to us" in Gadamer's quote tellingly discloses what we deem most important, most central, most germane.

I remember when I first saw the "Bizarro World" of the words in Romans 8 while preparing for that meeting with Jean where I asked her to engage in the exercise of breathing prayer. Crying, groaning, and sighing are not what human beings are aiming for in life; in fact, we would prefer exactly the opposite. I was much more familiar with the triumphal verses that conclude the chapter, verses 28–39. Those words do indeed soar from the confident, "We know that all things work together for good for those who love God, who are called according to his purpose," through the strident theological assertions of God's foreknowledge of us, God's predestination of us, and God's election of us, to the rapid-fire series of rhetorical questions that punctuate God's unflagging faithfulness to us, to the crescendo: "No, in all these things we are more than conquerors through him who loved us. For I am convinced that neither death, nor life, nor angels, nor rulers, nor things present, nor things to come, nor powers, nor height, nor depth, nor anything else in all creation, will be able to separate us from the love of God in Christ Jesus our Lord." The elation Paul expresses is palpable. It's the same kind of ecstatic punctuation mark that he makes in 1 Corinthians 15:54b–58 when he exclaims, "'Death has been swallowed up in victory.' 'Where, O death, is your victory? Where, O death, is your sting?' The sting of death is sin, and the power of sin is the law. But thanks be to God, who gives us the victory through our Lord Jesus Christ."

This eschatological truth that Paul asserts is only possible from an apocalyptic perspective of the perishable body having put on imperishability, the mortal body having put on immortality (1 Cor 15:53–54), an occurrence for which we yet wait. Paul would not likely march the halls of a children's cancer ward shouting out like a madman, "Where, O death, is your victory? Where, O death, is your sting?" But I do imagine him walking those halls, as an old, broken-down man, weeping with those who weep, holding in his arthritic hands the hands of dying children, embodying in his presence there his stubborn belief in the apocalyptic gospel that the risen Jesus had himself revealed to this dreary-looking old codger.

The assertions in verses 28–39 that weave theological and christological confessional statements together like a perfect rope do not, interestingly, make one mention of the Holy Spirit. Yet, according to verses 14–27, it is the Holy Spirit who confirms the truth of all these assertions concerning

Breathing Prayer: Learning the Language of the Spirit

God's love and inseparable presence, by means of the language of lament in the form of cries, groans, and sighs. It is indeed a Bizarro truth. Those oftentimes unintelligible utterances of the broken human spirit are remarkably, Paul affirms, witnesses of God's enduring presence in and with us, helping us to endure.

Our cries of "Abba! Father!" testify to the Spirit's comingling with our human spirit to confirm that we are God's children, and thus heirs with God's only begotten child—heirs of glory! Our groans connect us both with a groaning creation and also with God's gift to us of the first fruits of the Spirit—the resurrection first fruits—and mark us as God's children by means of adoption. That adoption marks our bodies as redeemed, and thus filled with hope, and something Paul calls "patience," though we might sometimes want to call that special pleading. Finally, our sighs are not the final resort of the emotionally fatigued, but evidence that athough we do not know how to pray or what to pray, the Spirit nevertheless has actively jumped in as intercessor and animator of the forlorn and the soul weary.

> Likewise the Spirit helps us in our weakness; for we do not know how to pray as we ought, but that very Spirit intercedes with sighs too deep for words. And God, who, who searches the heart, knows what is the mind of the Spirit, because the Spirit intercedes for the saints according to the will of God. (Rom 8:26–27)

That is a profound recasting of what appears to be the case. Our lost cause turns out to be a part God's greatest cause, the recasting, redemption, and rectification of all creation.

But now, Paul insists, we wait. If Paul is right that creation is in labor, that the New Humanity in Christ have been adopted yet have not quite been revealed as the true children of God, that our bodies are in an incomplete state of redemption, then we are sort of like a Polaroid picture whose image is slowly taking shape, slowly coming into appearance on the film paper as one waves it in the air. We are somewhere between the snapshot having just been taken by the photographer and the picture being fully developed with all the lines and colors clarified. Paul even suggests that creation itself eagerly longs and anticipates our impending revelation as the children of God, which further suggests that to the naked eye it is not evident. The exposure is incomplete, opaque. But just as a woman in the throes of labor cannot change her mind about having a baby, God's Kingdom and God's children are on the verge of being fully known, full realized, fully visible, fully alive.

PART 1—MEDITATIONS AND REFLECTIONS

The book of Psalms, which I call the speech teacher for faith, concludes in the final psalm with a triumphal burst of praise:

> Praise the Lord!
> Praise God in his sanctuary;
>   Praise him in his mighty firmament!
> Praise him for his mighty deeds;
>   Praise him according to his greatness!
> Praise him with trumpet sound;
>   Praise him with lute and harp!
> Praise him with tambourine and dance;
>   Praise him with strings and pipe!
> Praise him with clanging cymbals;
>   Praise him with loud clashing cymbals!
> Let everything that breathes praise the Lord!
> Praise the Lord! (Ps 150:1–6)

Clearly we have caught the psalmist on a good day. How does one wrap up such a collection of hymns, which all attempt to articulate honest faith in worship of God, even when that honesty sometimes requires outcry and lament, not praise? The final word, the psalmist declares by editorial fiat, is praise. When Jean came to me, unable to pray, I think what tortured her was the sense that she knew this was true; that our chief end as human beings is, as the catechism insists, "to glory God and enjoy him forever." But in her heart of hearts she also knew a polar truth: she could not. Agonizingly, she still had breath in her body, but she could not muster it to do, to serve, what she knew to be her greatest reason for being, the praise of God.

The vantage point that we share now, this side of God's act in Jesus' death and resurrection, injects hermeneutical insight into Psalm 150. On the one hand, from the lookout point of the apocalyptic gospel, the now-but-not-yet triumph of God over powers of evil and death, we can shout Psalm 150 with the same confidence that Paul shouts the triumphant rhetorical and mocking questions that the resurrection has emboldened him with in 1 Corinthians 15: "Where, O death is your victory? Where, O death, is your sting?"

Yet, on the other hand, our enactment of Psalm 150 today looks absurd in view of a world full of so much war, terror, exploitation, pain, and suffering. Indeed, to enact Psalm 150 in worship today must look to the world like a farce and an incongruity. It must look a lot like that little scene in the movie *The Apostle* where the runaway murderer turned minister and self-appointed apostle, played by Robert Duvall, tells his little flock in the

Breathing Prayer: Learning the Language of the Spirit

Louisiana bayou to turn in their Bibles to Psalm 150. As he reads the psalm, he asks whether or not any of the twelve people there have any of the things the psalm mentions so that they might use them to praise God right then and there. An old man pulls out a trumpet and blasts an off-key note. A woman we've come to know has numerous troubles raises up a tambourine and shakes it wildly. Two little boys jump into the center aisle and strum on their hopelessly out-of-tune toy guitars. The elderly man begins blaring out on the trumpet again. This is clearly no Carnegie Hall concert going on. It is a ragtag remnant of misfits led by a runaway criminal incarnating the last psalm, a wished-for reach through a tear-streaked and war-depleted world that runs more on despair than hope most days. It is the church at worship, looking like freak show, sounding more like a cacophony than a symphony, uttering words that sound absolutely crazy to any sane observer of this world's woes.

I was drawn to Psalm 150 as the concluding thought to this meditation not only because of its confessional absurdity and apocalyptic truth, but also because of the word "breathes" in the final verse of this final psalm. The psalm is driven by a relentless series of imperatives—commands—to praise God. Those addressed with this command are not specified, until the final verse: "Let everything that breathes praise the Lord!" Yet, as the story of Jean so agonizingly demonstrates, not everything that still has breath has the capacity to praise God, given the experiences of suffering and loss that each has endured.

In Romans 8 Paul address this dilemma by asserting that God's own Breath breathes through us with movements and articulations that God knows and understands. Our spirits, brokenhearted by this world's tragic fissures, utter cries, groans, and sighs, and by the grace, mercy, and providence of God they collaborate with God's Breath, God's Spirit, and ascend to God. The gospel is that even the impossible imperatives of Psalm 150 are taken up by God, articulated, and completed on our behalf.

PART 2

Proclaiming God's Reign in a World that Is Passing Away

5

The Widow's Plight: Redefining Stewardship via Justice-Making and Justice-Keeping

(Meditation, Reflection, and Proclamation on Mark 12:41–44)

A BLUE, JITTERY LIGHT emanated from the sixth floor window of a dirty, beaten-down apartment building. Someone was watching television late into the cold night. Its images jabbed the night sky. In the apartment, an elderly woman, alone since her husband died twelve years earlier, was watching a man in a light blue suit with comb-over hair passionately plead with her, and God knows how many others at that hour, to join him in spreading the gospel to the nations of the world who had never heard the good news. It did not matter how much she could give, he assured her; any amount was important.

The camera then cut to the man sitting casually in a wing chair by a fire. It felt like an intimate, one-on-one conversation now: "If you send in your financial contribution to help this ministry, we will be able to continue to do what we know God has put us on this planet to do—proclaim the gospel to all the nations." Then he threw his listeners a curve ball. "But if you do not, others will give, and we will still continue our ministry. The truth is, we don't really need your contribution; God will always raise up others to contribute if you do not respond to the call. But I am speaking to you now because I also know that if you send us a gift that truly challenges you, right now in your faith journey with God, then I know that God will see and know what you are doing, and you will be blessed by the one who sees you in secret. You see, this moment is an opportunity for you more than it is a fundraising moment for me and my ministry. And that's why I am so excited to be the ambassador of your faith opportunity. The amount you send us matters mostly to you and God. I know this because God will raise up the faith warriors we need to sustain our work. God has already promised me this. But this moment is about you. This moment is about you now and your faith journey; it is about you and your relationship with God! Will you be like the faithful widow in Mark's Gospel, who was willing to give everything she had to live on, her entire life, for God's sake, that God's work go on? Will you be praised by Jesus himself, just as she was, and lifted to the rafters of heaven as one of the shining saints that supported the spread of God's good news?!"

The woman stood up and went to her little desk in the corner of her small apartment and took the checkbook out of the top drawer. She looked at the ledger and saw $162.41 in the balance line. It was seven days before her next Social Security check would arrive, that $1,226 per month her sole means of sustenance. Convicted to join God's work with a display of faith like she never had before, she wrote out the check for all $162.41 to the ministry of the comb-over man in the blue suit, put it in the envelope, sealed it, put a "Forever" stamp on it, and immediately went to the street to put it in the mailbox before a potential lack of faith shook her back to her senses. Leaving her building, she pulled the corners of her coat up around her neck as she shuffled down the sidewalk. Reaching the box, she pulled open the door, put her letter in, and closed it. She opened it back up just to make sure it had gone all the way down. "Good," she thought to herself. She then exhaled a heavy sigh and walked back to her apartment.

The comb-over man in the blue suit may be the exception rather than the rule—thank God—but his slick rhetoric is but an exaggeration of a prevalent and pervasive problem in almost every ministry. Many churches have turned the problem into a season, "Stewardship Season," that culminates in a special Sunday, "Pledge Sunday," the hope being that congregational pledges will cover the budget projections for the upcoming fiscal year, or come close enough that weekly plate offerings might be able to cover the shortfall.

Stewardship Season exacts a keen pressure on pastoral staff in North American churches. Many church leaders urge their parishioners to practice the ancient spiritual discipline of tithing, giving 10 percent of their income to the church, even bringing to church an angry prophet named Malachi (3:8): "Will anyone rob God? Yet you are robbing me! But you say, 'How are we robbing you?' In your tithes and offerings!" Malachi is a convenient guest screamer and guilt producer on Pledge Sunday.

Redefining Stewardship via Justice-Making and Justice-Keeping

Debates rage, of course, about whether that 10 percent should be on one's net or gross income, but such squabbling is largely moot since statistics that track what parishioners actually give are startling, and make the debate about tithing net or gross purely academic. A recent study showed that the percentage of income that church members in North America are donating to the church is 2.3.[1]

In face of this, ministers scramble to creatively boost giving in order to meet expenses in the form of church property, staff compensation, missions, and denominational assessments and apportionments. The minister who must preach during Stewardship Season is always looking for some text that might spark a renewed sense of financial commitment to in the church. It's an increasingly tough sell among parishioners who have grown cynical toward all institutions, including the church. As one parishioner put it to me, "I have no problem giving my money to God for the work of building the Kingdom in this world. My problem is that I have to give through all these middlemen, and frankly, I don't trust them."

What's a preacher to do? Especially because there is a kind of special pleading going on in the stewardship sermon, since the preacher stands to benefit if things go well. Everyone knows this is an awkward situation. Enter the poor widow.

The widow is seemingly a godsend to the preacher. She has been hermeneutically chauffeured to church from her bare studio apartment every fall so she can wobble frailly to the front and drop her two pennies into the plate (with microphone carefully placed and turned up to amplify their clang through the Bose sanctuary speakers) in front of the awed preacher and congregation. She has been called the patron saint of Pledge Sunday. All year she waits for her moment, scraping together her offering from the non-existent excess of her Social Security checks. She is extolled as the perfect example of a generous giver. We preachers love her: *"She had so little, but gave so much." "If she, out of her poverty, could be so generous, how much more should we give generously out of our abundance?" "It must have hurt for her to dig so deep. Do you have faith to give till it hurts!?"* We are thrilled to have her come to church once a year to help us get through Stewardship Season. We are grateful to be able to homiletically hide behind her tattered dress and unkempt hairdo.

---

1. This was down from 2.4 percent in 2011. Burgess, "Church giving reaches Depression-era record lows."

But, as you can probably tell, I am uncomfortable with this arrangement. It is too convenient for us and too exploitative for her. In fact, I believe we must name this use of the widow for our fundraising needs a kind of exegetical abuse of the Markan story, and pastoral abuse of any "widow" who is guilted into giving by the story's misuse. Exegetical abuse, a form of textual harassment, can have social, political, and pastoral implications that constitute a compromise of the gospel. If the preacher was as concerned for the poor widow as he was for his budget shortfall, he might not be blinded by this seeming opportunity to guilt people into upping their annual giving to, Lord knows, maybe even 3 or 4 percent. Indeed, the preacher should be worried that an investigative team from *60 Minutes* might catch wind of this scam and show up asking questions, sending a camera crew over to the widow's empty-cupboard, electricity-and-water-turned-off apartment to show her dwindling away in her impoverishment while they show in a split-screen video the church's new family life center under construction, funded by the generous pledges that flowed in after our most successful Pledge Sunday to date.

There are social implications to the misuse of Scripture and its key characters. Because if we can make the widow in the text into an example for us to follow, then we can forget that, historically, theologically, and pastorally, the widow existed in Israelite culture as someone *for whom* the community was supposed to muster great amounts of caring energy rather than be a source of cash flow or an example of giving. If she is just an example of generous giving for Pledge Sunday, we can forget that she is our responsibility. And, by analogy, the "widows" of our day—the vulnerable in our midst who are without power, voice, or position—can be neglected too, or trotted out at, say, election time, as an example of our façade of compassionate conservatism, or an example of how our church cares for one impoverished family on the other side of the world. Tragically, we turn our present-day widows, orphans, and strangers in the land into advertisements for our fundraising attempts to extract contributions from stingy congregants rather than realizing that these real-life tragic situations of human need involve people in need for whom we, like the ancient temple leaders before us, are responsible and accountable. If we are going to use them this way, let's at least be honest with them ahead of time and promise them a percentage of the take.

The use of this text in the North American Christian preaching tradition affords us another reflective opportunity—one on the nature of

Redefining Stewardship via Justice-Making and Justice-Keeping

application, the hermeneutics of using a text from the past in a current context. It is my contention that the use of "The Widow's Mite" story in the preaching and teaching tradition of the church is a classic example of how the traditional use of a text blinds the eye of the interpreter from seeing anything other than what the interpreter has already seen. Abraham Heschel observed that this problem of "seeing," or thinking we know what we see when we look at a situation or text, is humankind's chief problem, and is, in fact, why God sent the prophets.

Heschel's assertion bears repeating: humankind's chief problem is that we think we know what we see. Heschel writes, "What impairs our sight are habits of seeing as well as the mental concomitants of seeing. Our sight is suffused with knowing, instead of feeling painfully the lack of knowing what we see."[2] Over time, people grow accustomed to looking at and perceiving things a certain way. Such perceptions become calcified, and rather than a perception or interpretation, those perceptions are then understood to simply be "the way things are." God's prophets—the true "seers"—unmask the idolatry of hardened perceptions.

Exegesis for preaching—the methodical study of a text from the Bible with the goal of understanding that text in its historical, literary, and theological context as well as achieving insight into our contemporary situation from the text's angle of vision—must be prophetic in the same sense. A hermeneutic of suspicion should attend every engagement of especially accepted textual readings and usages.

Taking Heschel's suspicion seriously, when we read a text we must become suspicious of our first inclinations for how the text is to be understood and used, especially if we find ourselves quickly defaulting to certain inclinations of interpretation and application that align with how we have always heard it and done it before. Constant default to the same reading and use creates an idol. A prophetic exegesis, on the other hand, says, "Question what you first see, or what you think you see." Exegesis in the prophetic mode is especially crucial when the person interpreting the text stands to benefit in some way from the text's use in the traditional mode. When the preacher chooses, for example, to depart from the lectionary on Pledge Sunday in order to bring the widow and her two copper coins into the pulpit, the hermeneutical suspicion meter ought to begin sounding an alarm and flashing red danger signals.

---

2. Heschel, *Prophets*, xiii.

Let's analyze this tendency of the preacher a little more closely. Reading through Mark's Gospel one early fall afternoon, the preacher sees Jesus in Jerusalem nearing his end, and getting into one conflict after another with the religious leaders. Then, after warning his disciples about the arrogant and socially manipulative scribes "who devour widow's houses," he then views an episode where a "poor" widow at the temple treasury is compared with "wealthy" temple goers. She is singled out by Jesus as giving more than all of them because she gave out of her poverty, "everything she had to live on," whereas they gave out of their abundance. The preacher's first inclination, with Stewardship Season looming, is to see Jesus praising her and seemingly making her an example of generous and sacrificial giving. The preacher thinks, "This is a perfect example-for-generous-giving text, especially for penny-pinching, tightfisted congregants. Save it for Pledge Sunday."

Exegesis in the prophetic vein would say, "Hold on, preacher, slow down. That's the way you've always seen it, preached it, and heard it preached, but is your knowing impairing your capacity to see what may really be there?" Heschel would ask, "Is your seeing suffused with too much knowing?" Hans Georg Gadamer would ask, "Have the prejudices from your uncritically examined interpretive horizon (not to mention your need to exact pledges to meet pressing budget demands) put a cloud in front of the horizon of the text and its potential prophetic demands?"[3] If, in fact, this text were doing the opposite of what you think, and was in fact prophetically calling your congregation to identify, rescue, and care for people in your social context that were as used and abused as this poor widow, would you still use it for stewardship season?

Philosopher Ludwig Wittgenstein drew a duck and showed some people his simple drawing. They saw a duck. Then he turned the image to illustrate that if they looked at the picture from a different starting point they would see a rabbit. *Voila!* It was a rabbit, not a duck! Wait, was it? Well, it was either a duck or a rabbit, but it couldn't be both at the same time.[4]

When we read the story of the widow in Mark we make several assumptions that are, as Heschel would say, the "mental concomitants" of our stubborn knowing. We assume Jesus is praising the widow, but is he, or is that our agenda? We assume that he is pointing to her as an ideal example

---

3. Gadamer, *Truth and Method*, 269–70, 360–62. For Gadamer, the tradition equips us with the hermeneutical prejudices necessary to see what we receive from the tradition. Yet, blindness to what we have received can result in hidden prejudices that can cloud our reception of the tradition.

4. Wittgenstein, *Philosophical Investigations*, book 2, section xi.

Redefining Stewardship via Justice-Making and Justice-Keeping

of giving, but is he, or is he simply contrasting her giving with that of others with a view to revealing what God knows that humans do not? We assume that he's telling a story of giving to the temple, and all it represents as the institutional religion of the time, as being a good and laudatory thing, but is he, especially given what he is in Jerusalem to do?

Elements that would make this a praise-and-example text are missing, namely Jesus saying something like, "Blessed is she," "Go and do likewise," "Because she has done this she has stored up treasure in heaven," or "Wherever the church achieves 100 percent tithing among its members, this story will be told in memory of her." In fact, all that Jesus does is report what he sees and what he knows. He says, "This is the truth: that widow put in the most of everyone. They contributed out of their abundance; she out of her poverty. She put in everything she had to live on" (my paraphrase). We normally hear and say Jesus' words with a lilt in his expression, to make him sound like he's happy and commending her as an example. That could have a powerful effect on parishioners who would like God's approval for their generous giving. Some suggest he's even winking and moving his shoulder toward her as if to say, "Now you see what she did? That's the way it ought to be done, yes siree!" We add the tone and the body language because we have to in order to get the text to bow to our desired function.

However, in preparing to read aloud—better, orally perform—this text in the worship assembly, what clues can we find *in* the text and its context to help us to perform it in a manner commensurate with the text as we have it? Interestingly, the traditional use of this story in fundraising attempts requires no attention to context, and may in fact depend on remaining blind to its context, which, when examined, enables us to see the story quite differently.

What might we learn from attending to the immediate literary context? The Jerusalem section in Mark's Gospel begins in 11:1, when Jesus rode into the city on a colt. The fanfare is short-lived as Jesus goes immediately into the temple. He is casing the place, and Mark tells us that because it was late in the day Jesus left. The next day, however, we are not left wondering what Jesus' assessment of the temple was. In Markan literary fashion, he narrates Jesus' judgment and thrashing of the temple between his telling of Jesus' cursing of a fig tree. The fig tree's cursing and subsequent withering away to its roots are the "bread" of the Markan sandwich around the "meat" of the temple's so-called cleansing. The message is clear: Jesus is on the scene at the temple and in Jerusalem to curse it to its fruitless roots. To Jesus, the temple and its leadership have lost their God-compass, and instead have become economically driven and self-serving. His first act in Jerusalem is the condemnation of the temple by driving out (Greek = *ekballo*, the same word used in Mark for Jesus' exorcisms of demons from people) the merchants who were buying and selling and overturning the tables of the money changers, with this indictment from their own Scriptures: "Is it not written, 'My house shall be called a house of prayer for all the nations'? But you have made it a *den of robbers*" (Mark 11:17).

What follows is a series of conflict stories between Jesus and the Jerusalem leadership, causing escalating tension that leads up to a specific warning about the scribes. In the episode immediately preceding the widow's mite story, Jesus warns his disciples about the scribes and the abuse of their position, especially their economic violation of the vulnerable widows: "Beware of the scribes who like to walk around in long robes, and to be greeted with respect in the marketplaces, and to have the places of honor at banquets! *They devour widows' houses* and for the sake of appearance say long prayers. They will receive the greater condemnation" (Mark 12:38–40, emphasis added).

Jesus criticizes the scribes for selfish vanity in social circumstances and for using a show of prayer to promote their appearance of piety, but arguably the greatest accusation he makes against them, and the only one that could bring them up on charges that could hold them criminally liable, is the claim that they fraudulently exploit the financial assets of that already fragile sector of their community, widows. This indictment of the scribes by Jesus was more than saying that they were talking these women into questionable reverse mortgages. The Greek word translated as "devour," *katesthio*, is an aggressive term, used in other contexts to refer to the way birds and even dragons eat their prey. It is a term that implies a gobbling up of another, or in this case another's property, by force, and because of an insatiable and amoral appetite that has no regard or concern for the other.[5]

In the episode immediately following the widow's mite story, Mark tells us that the disciples are enamored with the grandeur of the temple and its impressive stonework. Apparently, Jesus isn't as impressed. He says, "Do you see these great buildings? Not one stone will be left here upon another; all will be thrown down" (Mark 13:2).

Jesus was on the scene in Jerusalem for the express purpose of taking down the temple and its corruption, a corruption that stooped so low that

---

5. Bauer, Arendt, and Gingrich, *Lexicon*, "*katesthio*," 422.

it would take advantage of widows and what could be their only and final asset, their homes. His primary beef with the temple scribes had to do with their greedy use of the temple, and apparently anyone they could manipulate, for their own financial gain.

With the widow's mite story falling right between his judgment of the scribes for "devouring widows' houses" and the indictment of and predicted future demise (which for Mark's readers would probably have already taken place) of a particularly economically predatory temple cult, one would have to posit that the story of a widow giving everything she had to live on to such people, and such a corrupt system, might be a lament rather than a praise.

Two further matters command our interpretive consideration. First, Jesus uses a comparison in this story that has led some to conclude that he is thus exhibiting the widow as an example of how to give in contrast to the wealthy people who do not. The widow put in *"more than"* everyone else. What was the reason for this comparison? They contributed out of abundance, but she out of poverty. The fact of the comparison does not, however, mean that he is lifting her up as an example for anyone to follow. Rather, the point seems to be that mere human perception cannot see what is really going on here. Only God can see that her contribution, because it is a greater percentage of her net worth, is in actuality a greater amount—a more costly amount—than anyone else's, even though it appears to be less because it is only two thin copper coins. Thus, the text is more an indictment of the wealthy and the human proclivity toward using situations of perception, especially as they pertain to giving assets to the religious institution, to deceive and gain clout (see Acts 5:1–11).

In the context, however, both historically and literarily, his observation of her "greater giving" is to be taken, I maintain, as a lament of her treatment and an indictment of a system that would perpetuate such abuse of the most vulnerable members of the community.[6] Joel Marcus, who disagrees with my reading, nevertheless asks, "Why, then, does Mark place her story precisely here, between the excoriation of ravenous scribes and the prophecy of the Temple's destruction? It may be that he does so unconscious of the jangling elements in the context, intent only on the pericope's central message of the importance of whole-hearted devotion and the literary necessity of placing it in a 'Temple' section."[7]

---

6. See Marcus, *Mark 8–16*, 857–63, for a counter opinion.
7. Ibid., 862–63.

The "jangling elements in the context" are resolved, however, if the interpreter attributes Mark's careful placement of the story precisely here in order to focus on one of his central messages in the entire Jerusalem narrative: *indicting the scribes and the temple leaders for economic injustice*. In fact, rather than considering Mark "unconscious of the jangling elements" of his placement of the story of the widow right here, my interpretation ascribes a highly conscious placement that points to Mark's narrative genius and artistry.

Second, widows in our day and age often do not fit the same category that they did in Mark's. They were usually destitute and dependent on the community, while today they are often financially independent. The correlative in our world, therefore, for the preacher to explore, would be any group of people who, due to societal and religious marginalization, are highly vulnerable and susceptible to financial manipulation and extortion. This could be actual widows, but such a characterization widens the lens for those who would fit the category of victims of economic injustice.

In turn, what might we learn from the historical and theological context? For Mark's Gospel, that means that we engage in what I call a prophetic perspective and reading. That is because Mark's historical and theological context is primarily that of Israel's scriptures, especially as they are accessed through Mark's prophetic vision. Jesus' hidden messianic presence in Mark gains visibility primarily through the lens of the prophetic. Mark explicitly begins his Gospel narrative out of the prophetic vision in 1:2: "As it is written in the prophet Isaiah . . ." Jesus was thought to be a prophet by many in Mark's narrative, and Jesus, in self-reference, uses a proverb regarding the precariousness of being a prophet in one's own home town (6:4, 15; 8:28). A prophetic interpretive approach examines Jesus' every act and word with careful scrutiny to the way the text helps us discern what matters most to God in human social situations, especially in situations where power dynamics are involved.

One of the distinctive features of Israelite religion and culture, as evidenced in the Old Testament, was the constant emphasis on God's special concern for justice-making and justice-keeping—a concern that demanded periodic exposures of injustice. Whatever atrocities God saw in the human social landscape became the "burden" (Hebrew *massah*, often translated "oracle") of God's chosen prophet. This explains the visual metaphors that are associated with the prophets. They are "seers." Their oracles/burdens derive from visions that God makes them see: "The vision of Isaiah, son of

Redefining Stewardship via Justice-Making and Justice-Keeping

Amoz, which he saw" (Isa 1:1); "... as I was among the exiles... the heavens were opened, and I saw the visions of God... as I looked... as I looked... When I saw it, I fell on my face..." (Ezek 1:1, 4, 15, 28); "The words of Amos... which he saw..." (Amos 1:1); "The vision of Obadiah..." (Obad 1:1); "The word of the Lord that came to Micah... which he saw..." (Mic 1:1); "The book of the vision of Nahum..." (Nah 1:1); "The oracle [*massah*, burden] that Habakkuk the prophet saw" (Hab 1:1). Most often the socially atrocious situations are due to the misuse of power that results in extreme economic injustice toward the most vulnerable, those with the least recourse to legal rectification. Only someone who had nothing to lose, and who was accountable to no human authority, could call the powerful upper-class leadership to account for such malfeasance, when such calling to account would have potentially dire consequences for the exposer. This is what made the prophets so dangerous. Commissioned to *say* what God *sees*, the prophets called for justice and made it clear that God loves justice, especially for that triad of characters that encapsulated the most vulnerable: the widow, the orphan, and the stranger in the land. God's love—obsession even—for justice was to be the number-one priority above all other qualities in leadership in the community.

It is this prophetic predisposition—the preloading of one's reading with the backdrop of God's predilection for justice, especially as that extends to the poor and at-risk defenseless—that the interpreter of Mark's Gospel must bring to the text if it is to be understood aright. Someone might object, "But isn't that eisegesis, the bringing of a presupposition from outside the text and plopping it down into the middle of this text?" My answer is, "Yes, it is, but it is good eisegesis." Not all eisegesis is created equal.

Eisegesis has gotten a bad rap by some who teach exegesis courses primarily because they often caricature it as the arm-wrestling of a given text to mean what the interpreter wants it to mean without regard for what the text is actually trying to say. This kind of poor eisegesis should rightly be cautioned against. However, another kind of so-called eisegesis takes place when preachers come to any given text with the call to preach the gospel in conversation with a given text.

Reading Scripture for preaching the gospel is inherently eisegetical, but not in the bad or distorting way ordinarily chastised, because it consists of a creative conversation between the preacher's working understanding of the gospel and the claims and impulses of the text itself. Most preachers know that their primary call is to preach the gospel. It is also the case that most preachers realize that any given text served up in the Bible may not contain or bear witness to the preacher's working gospel. It is in the creative conversation between the preacher's working gospel, the biblical text at hand, and the concrete situation that the preacher is addressing that the sermon emerges. Thus the preacher not only brings his or her working gospel to the text, but also the congregational context and whatever issues need to be engaged by both gospel and text.

When one's working gospel is shaped especially by the prophetic perspective that accentuates God's special concern for the widow, orphan, and stranger in the land, our text in question, Mark 12:38–42, the widow's mite story, becomes a case in point for a prophetic reading.

First, as noted earlier, it's clear that from the moment Jesus steps foot in Jerusalem he's not happy with the way the temple has lost its God-compass and has instead become economically driven and self-serving. His first act in Jerusalem is to condemn the temple, driving out (literally, "exorcising") the money changers with the indictment that they had turned God's "house of prayer" into a "den of robbers" (11:17).

Second, a prophetic reading also proceeds by being suspicious of institutions, because institutions typically become self-serving and overly concerned with their own survival. Those who make their way up the food chain in the institution increasingly benefit from the institution's economic success, which makes them questionable critics of the institution and usually defensive, even kneejerk supporters of it. The ongoing demands of overhead in religious properties ("Look at these large stones!" "We are already half way to our goal for breaking ground on the family life center!") exert themselves in the practice of partiality: the favoring of congregants at the "top" who have wealth, position, power, and status, and the neglecting of the people at the "bottom" who have nothing to offer the institution but problems and needs. The "bottom people" are seen as a drain on the institution's energy and assets. Any mention of the temple and its leaders in a text would signal to one reading with prophetic eyes something significant, and it should put on notice any contemporary leaders of present day "temples" that they had better be careful.

Third, if preachers come to Mark 12 from a prophetic perspective, alarms would start ringing the moment their eyes fall on the word "widow," since it is functionally a technical term in biblical literature. Moreover, it's not as if the term is only casually introduced into the narrative. After driving out the money changers from the temple, and after criticizing the

Redefining Stewardship via Justice-Making and Justice-Keeping

scribes' temple leadership as theologically bankrupt and economically self-serving, Jesus then levels this charge against them: they economically ruin widows, those among them who are most economically vulnerable. Very cleverly, they have turned the drain on their resources into a pipeline of income, modest as it is.

Fourth, Mark tells us that Jesus situates himself across from where temple-goers would put their offerings. He observes many rich people putting in large sums of money. Then a poor widow comes up. She is not just a widow but, according to Mark, a *poor* widow. She puts in her offering. It isn't a tithe, a mere 10-percent offering. It's everything she has to live on, her entire *bios* ("life"), 100 percent of her assets and existence! Is that what the Law asks of her? Is that what God wants of anyone, other than perhaps a rich person whose riches are keeping him from true discipleship (Mark 10:21)?

Jesus is here saying to his disciples, in light of everything that he's said, done, and will do in Jerusalem, "Do you see what I mean about scribes and widows? There goes another poor widow down the tubes."

It didn't look like much. To everyone else it seemed like business as usual at the place where people gave their offerings to the temple. This poor widow was in and out without notice, just like they probably never noticed anything she ever did. Her contribution wouldn't even make a dent in the budget. It was probably even an annoyance, those two virtually worthless coins. But Jesus sees and Jesus knows. Jesus has been aiming at Jerusalem for arguably the entire Gospel narrative, and if he needed any added incentive to fulfill his mission, he had it here.

In Jesus, God is on the scene to bring down the very system that the widow gave her whole life to. God recognizes that even in the middle of corrupt and entrenched religious systems there are still the pure of heart who are doing the best that they know how to do but know of no other way to God than through the official system, as suspect as it may appear to be. Contrasting the enormity of her giving with that of the rich people, Jesus may praise her devotion to God in comparison to theirs, but his observation is at the same time a lament of a system that would permit, codify, and encourage such widow abuse.

What do I mean by saying that "widow" is a technical term in the biblical literature? A concordance search reveals this:

> You shall not abuse any widow or orphan. If you do abuse them, when they cry out to me, I will surely heed their cry; my wrath

will burn, and I will kill you with the sword, and your wives shall become widows and your children orphans. (Exod 22:22–24)

The Lord your God is God of gods and Lord of lords, the great God, mighty and awesome, who is not partial and takes no bribe, who executes justice for the orphan and the widow, and who loves the strangers, providing them food and clothing. (Deut 10:17)

You shall not deprive a resident alien or an orphan of justice; you shall not take a widow's garment in pledge. Remember that you were a slave in Egypt and the Lord your God redeemed you from there, therefore I command you from there, therefore I command you to do this. (Deut 24:17–18)

When you have finished paying all the tithe of your produce in the third year (which is the year of the tithe), giving it to the Levites, the aliens, the orphans, and the widows, so that they may eat their fill within your towns, then you shall say before the Lord your God: "I have removed the sacred portion from the house, and have given it to the Levites, the resident aliens, the orphans, and the widows, in accordance with your entire commandment that you have commanded me; I have neither transgressed nor forgotten any of your commandments." (Deut 26:12–13)

Wash yourselves; make yourselves clean; remove the evil of your doings from before my eyes; cease to do evil, learn to do good; seek justice, rescue the oppressed, defend the orphans, plead for the widow. (Isa 1:16–17)

Thus says the Lord, "Act with justice and righteousness, and deliver from the hand of the oppressor anyone who has been robbed. And do no wrong or violence to the alien, the orphan or the widow, or shed innocent blood in this place." (Jer 22:3)

The word of the Lord came to Zechariah, saying: "Thus says the Lord of hosts: Render true judgments, show kindness and mercy to one another, do not oppress the widow, the orphan, the alien, or the poor; and do not devise evil in your hearts against one another." (Zech 7:8–10)

Redefining Stewardship via Justice-Making and Justice-Keeping

> Religion that is pure and undefiled before God, the Father, is this: to care for the orphans and the widows in their distress, and to keep oneself unstained by the world. (Jas 1:27)

According to these texts, the implication is that not only were widows not to give *all* they had to the temple, as the widow in Mark's story did, they were not even supposed to tithe. In fact, *they were not supposed to give anything at all* because they were supposed to be recipients of the offerings collected by the temple treasury.

In its literary, historical, theological, and prophetic context, we are given the clues to this text's import: it is the antithesis of an example-forgiving text. Jesus' warning echoes through this text: "Beware of the scribes for they devour widows' houses.... And there goes another one down the tubes of the religious establishment's neglect and greed."

The bad news in this episode seems clear. Is there any good news? There is, I believe, an ironic good news present here, as is frequently the case in Mark. In fact, this story is itself an apocalyptic preface to the "little apocalypse" of chapter 13, for it is a *revelation* of a seemingly innocuous moment in the life of the temple, yet through the eyes of Jesus a moment that (1) reveals a widow's life sacrifice (foreshadowing Jesus' own life sacrifice), (2) reveals the extent of the scribes' corruption, neglect, and lawlessness, and (3) provides one more reason why this seemingly impressive structure and system (Mark 13:1) must be obliterated (13:2; 15:38).

This is a good news that is truly startling to behold. Mark takes the risk to portray a religious system and religious leaders who are corrupt and rotten to the core, abusive to those who are most pure of heart and vulnerable, neglectful and disrespectful of the very people they were meant to serve and care for, and blinded by their own greed and lust for popularity and power. But in spite of all this God is nevertheless on the scene: God, in the person of Jesus, sees, exposes, and does not abandon the vulnerable forever to such venality. In the hidden King/Messiah Jesus, God is on the scene to take stock and control, even when no one else sees, knows, or cares. God even knows the hearts and motives of those who are doing their best within hopeless structures. God sees and knows those who are using the systems to their own ends, to advance their own earthly, temporal careers, their own political agendas, their own lusts and greed. God knows the true score, and God is on the scene to do something decisive about it. In Mark's Gospel, Jesus is in Jerusalem to take it down and put in place an alternative that better reflects God's will and way, the Reign of God.

PART 2—PROCLAIMING GOD'S REIGN IN A WORLD THAT IS PASSING AWAY

This should give us—the church and its leaders—both hope and humility, as well as courage to hold course while God brings about God's ultimate rectification. If you are like me, you have been reluctant at times to give to churches and parachurch helping organizations because you knew too much about those in the leadership positions. Jesus, however—the one who sees, reveals, and knows—goes to Jerusalem, to the temple, and like the widow offers his life—his *bios*—for its ransom (Mark 10:45).

Ironically, this story about the widow ends up being a stewardship text after all, and maybe even an example text. But it isn't the widow and her giving all her money that is our example to follow. It's Jesus. We cannot always redeem our corrupt institutions, but we can give ourselves to the service of the prophetic gospel within them—naming the injustices, unmasking the idolatries, and proclaiming in the face of abusive power God's alternative will and way—trusting that God is still present, has not abandoned us, and is still working toward an ultimate justice and righteousness within our institutions and often in spite of them.

This is a stewardship text because it reminds us that though the widow is a victim here of an off-kilter religious system, if we were to tilt it back to on-kilter we would remember that we are a community charged with the responsibility for the care and sustenance of the most vulnerable and powerless among us. The widow, orphan, and stranger in the land are not drains on our budget. They are a primary reason why the church exists at all. Because the widow, orphan, and stranger give the church the opportunity to be the ark of compassion, support, and care, they need to experience something of the *shalom*, the human flourishing, that God created humans for and that he recreated them in Christ to finally realize.

In Jesus' vision of the Kingdom of God, everyone has a place at God's table and everyone brings something to contribute. As with the oft-named biblical triad—the widow, the orphan, and the stranger—what some bring to the table is only need, a fact that helps those who have an abundance of resources remember what they are there for.

Abraham Heschel said that God sends prophets because humanity's seeing is suffused with too much knowing. The prophets identify the self-serving ways and self-preserving structures that institutions put in place to justify their neglect of the poor and vulnerable. Maybe another aspect of the good news of this text is that God continues to send such prophets to call us to account, and intriguingly those prophets often take the form of our contemporary widows, orphans, and strangers in the land. It is their

Redefining Stewardship via Justice-Making and Justice-Keeping

presence among us that ought to make our prophetic alarms ring loudly in our often-deaf ears.

Who has eyes to really see? Who has ears to really hear? Who is not so entangled in institutional politics that their eyes are blinded to seeing how we keep justifying our neglect of today's widows, to see that we keep creating and maintaining structures and processes that work directly against the core values of God's Kingdom?

On that day at the temple when the poor widow had her house gobbled up in the presence of all those who had come to worship, no one noticed but Jesus. No one else cared. Where were the stewards of the treasury when she needed to be stopped in her attempt to give? Why had they not been visiting her regularly before then so she would not have even been the object of Jesus' lament that day?

O God, give us eyes to see and ears to hear, that our knowing might be overwhelmed by a new seeing; that the whispers of your prophets among us might rouse us from the slumber of our self-serving neglect and abuse of the vulnerable and needy. Help us to see the widow today and give us courage to dismantle whatever oppresses her, even if what must be dismantled are our own beloved institutions, the idolatrous overhead of our bloated religious facilities, and our own hard-fought-for-and-won positions of power and authority. Amen.

6

Casting Our Mammon on the Baptismal Waters:

Preaching Economic Justice in Lent

Lent's Gospel Resources

THE SEASONS OF THE church year, illumined as they are by the narrative portrayal of Jesus' life and ministry in the Gospels, provide continual light for Christians to examine their lives and commitments. Lent situates us at a crucial juncture in that story: the unrelenting and unchangeable path to the cross. When Ash Wednesday hits, we are at Luke 9:51 and there is no going back: "When the days drew near for him to be taken up, he set his face to go to Jerusalem." As Christians we are drop-shipped directly from baptism onto this Lenten road.

Water is an element that I love and fear. There is nothing like the feeling of diving into and through a crisp, salty ocean wave. Warm water gently embraces and soothes the aching body even as it cleanses. Pouring pure, cool water down a parched throat gives a kind of relief that is singular in life. At the same time, one of the most stressful nightmares I've ever had was of being in an underwater tunnel unable to find my way to the surface. My despair at the prospect of drowning woke me. Baptism holds both the thrill of life and the terror of death in creative tension, especially in those traditions that regularly practice baptism by immersion. I grew up in such a tradition.

When I was eight years old, I stood in the baptistery of a little church in Oceanside, California, having responded to the invitation to baptism that capped the Sunday evening sermon. The minister, Eugene Winters, whispered to me, "Hold your nose with your fingers or water will go up it when I tip you back." After he said those words, everything went into slow motion as I fell back into the chilly water. I opened my eyes on the way back up, thinking, "I don't want to miss anything of what this newly resurrected life looks like." I remember how pure, clean, and untainted by sin I felt at the moment. (Heady thoughts for an eight-year-old, I know.) Reflecting the preaching and teaching I had heard my whole life, I thought that my first sin would undo the whole thing. When I would later study about the Essenes and their daily baptismal ritual, I thought I understood where they were coming from. What a great idea to have a daily sin-rinse ritual! As I grew in my understanding of baptism over the years, however, I realized that my baptismal moment in May 1966 was one that I would never really be done with, any more than it would be done with me. Lent insistently reminds us that baptism, by the mystery of God's stubborn grace, is never done with us.

Historically, Lent is the season of preparation for baptism by initiates to the Christian faith, and of renewal of baptismal graces and commitments by those continuing their faith journeys in Christ. Whether we were baptized as infants, children, young adults, or in mature adulthood, Lent leads us back to the river, whether literal, metaphorical, or both, and invites us to wade back into the cleansing and renewing tide of God's mercy. Lent takes us to the water and says, "This is where you began. This is where God birthed you anew. This is where the death of Jesus and your impending death collided. This is where you died to ways contrary to God's designs for you. This is where the hem of Jesus' resurrection garment brushed up against you and you received power to rise up out of your watery grave into a life as you never knew it before. By God's miraculous and mysterious working, these waters washed you, purified you, and set you apart—sanctified you, made you holy—for God's purposes in the world. These waters immersed you into the fathomless love of God. They plunged you into God's will and way for as long as you have life, which is forever. This was your real birth, and when the water broke and you came forth as a new creation in Christ, you were no longer your own. You came forth God's person and God's possession, with all the privileges and responsibilities thereto appertaining."

When we all emerged from the baptismal maternity ward, we discovered something remarkable: we were not alone. We were now part of a family as large, as old, and as diverse as the human family. Our old world had been demarcated by lines around countries that told us our citizenry, by surnames that told us who our people were, but now those lines and ways of naming parentage and familial relations were gone. Our family resemblance now was based in God's image, and our citizenry by the Kingdom of God. Lent gives us all the chance to reconnect to our beginning and reminds us that by this new birth we have been organically joined to our divine, heavenly Parent and God's chosen and redeemed human family. I like what Martin Luther said when he was faced with difficult moments. He could always lean back as a final resort into the fact that "I am baptized," and know that God ultimately held him no matter what circumstance he encountered.

Preaching in Lent taps into the gospel resources that are available in baptism. Indeed, a good theology of baptism can resolve a lot of church problems. The Apostle Paul showed us that by frequently taking the readers and listeners of his letters back to their baptisms in order to reframe their consciousness and thus resolve church conflicts. Lent provides the time and space—forty days plus Sundays—for preachers to delve into the rich thematic depths of holiness, repentance, conversion, and the nature of discipleship. Concrete practices of spirituality punctuate the season's visual and verbal cues: the imposition of ashes, fasting, prayer, renewed meditation on Scripture and devotional resources, penitential acts, evangelism, efforts at justice-making and justice-keeping, and almsgiving. This last discipline, almsgiving, puts us in touch with our special concern for this reflection: the economics of Lenten discipleship.

Acoustical Armor: Hearer Resistance to Just Preaching

Preaching on economic justice requires several things of the preacher: a biblical and theological perspective on economics and justice, a political and sociological perspective on the current global economy, the gift and ability to prepare and deliver sermons, and, perhaps most important of all, sheer guts. This is because preaching on economics, politics, and justice matters can get you seriously injured if not killed. The prophets never got parades, at least not from the home crowd. The prophets always appeared to be cheering on the wrong sideline.

In his story "The Prophet,"[1] Garrison Keillor reveals how one July 4th God gave him the opportunity to be a prophet. Though only a child at the time, Keillor knew instantly that prophecy was not a career path he wanted

---

1. Featured in Keillor, *Lake Wobegon U.S.A.*

anything to do with. He did not want any part of a community role that would require him to become the scourge of the very people with whom he lived. So instead of becoming a prophet, one who told people the hard truth "that they had been successfully avoiding" and was then ostracized for it, Keillor decided to do the exact opposite. That's why, he explains, he chose to become a professional liar, one who weaves miles and miles of deception about a place and people who do not really exist. And ironically, he notes, since he became a professional liar he has been welcomed into as many pulpits from coast to coast as he wishes to speak, as often as he wishes. Whereas if he had chosen to take God up on the offer to become a prophet, Keillor would have been barred from most churches and pulpits throughout the country.

This tells preachers something about what they are up against when approaching a complicated, highly personal, and prophetic issue like money and justice. True prophets of God, like master artists, are only canonized after they're long dead and gone. My hunch is that Hananiah (the prophet whose popular sermon series on peace was rudely interrupted by the invasion and plunder of Jerusalem—see Jeremiah 28) would always get more ministry job offers than Jeremiah. In general, people love feel-good sermons that inspire them to lives that they are already comfortable with, but they get edgy and uncomfortable with sermons that meddle into "personal" and "private" matters like money, politics, and—surprise, surprise—even religion, especially when religion is described by the preacher as a not-so-private affair after all. Ruggedly individualistic American Christians grow especially antsy when the preacher calls on James' public version of true piety: "Religion that is pure and undefiled before God is this: to care for orphans and widows in their distress, and to keep oneself unstained by the world" (Jas 1:27). Most Christians who take their faith seriously would concur with the Presbyterian slogan that we are "reformed and always reforming," but the hard truth is that the social and economic reformation in thinking and living that prophets call people to is almost always resisted, and sometimes quite vigorously.

The church has invented a lot of excuses for its resistance, many of which are quite clever and even persuasive. The church has developed a talent for coming up with what looks like legitimate reasons for avoiding justice issues, or at least for letting them slip to the bottom of the priority list. These excuses can be categorized as theological, spiritual, ideological, and sociological.

Theologically, the church—especially the conservative church in all denominations—has conveniently avoided this-world justice concerns by an almost inordinate focus on the more important matters of "salvation and justification," especially as those matters are spiritualized and removed from the nitty-gritty matters of every day materiality. "Justice" in this mode of thinking is typically reduced to the appeasement of an angry God from whom we are estranged, with whom we need some form of atonement, an angry God who nevertheless arranges for us to be forgiven by means of the cruel sacrifice of his own sinless child. God's call for justice as a social and relational virtue and mandate among all peoples and the created order is mutated into humankind's need for a spiritualized righteousness achievable only by sacrifice on Jesus' part and faith on ours.[2] In this scenario the church's mission is reduced to evangelizing the lost in order to secure for them an afterlife in heaven. Focus on the then (afterlife) and there (heaven) makes any concern for the here and now seem less than truly Christian. Since nothing is more important than people's eternal destiny, undue attention to anything in this world is an unnecessary distraction from the church's priority to seek and save the lost.

This version of justice avoidance becomes most sinister when the ostensibly evangelistically focused church insists that only its version of and procedures for securing salvation are legitimate. William Muehl lampooned a justification-stuck ecclesiological mission in his sermon "The Cult of the Publican."[3] He illustrated the ultimate failure of the revivalists in the story of his uncle, a bar owner, who loved to tell about his six conversion experiences that resulted from the fire-and-brimstone preaching of Billy Sunday. But then, not recognizing his theological conundrum, his uncle would say, "But then every Monday there was this damn bar."[4] Exclusive attention to justification, even if well intentioned, without taking the next and necessary steps to a life of sanctification, and thus concrete actions for social righteousness in this world, must be named for what it is: heresy.

Spiritually, the church—especially the evangelical church—has conveniently reduced the life of faith to individualized piety. This causes faith to devolve into a head-in-the-sand, ostrich type of spirituality that is individualistic and sometimes even hedonistically self-centered and self-serving. Popular church music reinforces this form of spirituality with such

---

2. See Heim, *Saved from Sacrifice*, and Weaver, *Non-Violent Atonement*.
3. Muehl, "Cult of the Publican," 148.
4. Ibid.

hymns as "I Go to the Garden Alone," a hymn that extols the privatized, personal Savior who "walks with me and talks with me and tells me I am his own." Undue fixation on the privatized, personalized, individualized, retreat-to-the-hills-alone kind of Christian faith eclipses the sense of community interconnectedness and interdependence that is inherent to being God's people. Even our English translations of the Bible have been abused when plural second-person pronouns—"you"—are largely read, heard, interpreted, and internalized as singular pronouns, thus focused on the individual rather than the community. This is especially true with regard to the Pauline letters, where Paul's strong emphasis on community is lost when his plural "you" is read as a singular. Such privatization of spirituality must be named for what it is: heresy.

Ideologically, the church—especially the mainline church—has confused its ecclesial sense of self in the United States context with capitalism, democracy, and Americanism. It has preferred this cultural distortion of its ecclesiology over a more difficult and reflective evaluation of its surrounding cultural ideologies in light of the core theological categories of the cross, the spirit, and biblical perspectives on justice and love. The church thus violates its charter by allowing provincial ideologies to obscure its theology and faith. A recent example of this kind of distortion occurred when, after the terror attacks of 9/11, the American flag became a more important symbol for people than the cross, even in church sanctuaries. It almost goes without saying that the pledge of allegiance to the U.S. flag is a more important creed for many, if not most, American Christians than the Apostles' or Nicene Creeds, and that the national anthem evokes more emotion and passion than the hymn "God of Grace and God of Glory."

Greed is not only one of the seven deadly sins, but it is an ideology that the church has become quite tolerant of. As the character Gordon Gecko said in the movie *Wall Street*, "Greed is good." We might not be so crass as to confess that out loud, but the principle holds as an unspoken manifesto for many churchgoers. Especially as the wealth and prosperity gap widens, American Christians are having a harder and harder time evaluating the ideology and ethics of greed built on the economics of capitalism from the vantage point of Christian discipleship and stewardship. Much energy in recent decades has been expended in various sexual ethics debates, but I am convinced that greed exacts a greater moral cost in human relations, locally and globally. I often wonder what the twelve-year-old child on the other side of the globe thinks when, for twenty-two cents an hour, she cobbles together toys and knickknacks to be sold in so-called Old Country Stores to bored customers shopping while they wait for their tables to be ready. Our near complete silence in Christian pulpits on the problem of greed and its contribution to national and global economic injustice must be named for what it is: sin.

Sociologically, the American church has made a not-so-subtle shift in the questions it asks itself as it defines its mission in society. This shift has been influenced by the American market economy and the gluttonous desire to grow numerically at virtually any cost. Questions for the church's mission in this mode often start from a marketing frame of reference rather than a theological one. This change in orientation causes the church to change its basic question for mission from, "Given who we are as the biblical God's chosen people, the God who has a special concern for the most vulnerable in this world—the widow, the orphan, and the stranger in the land—how do we faithfully live out that identity in concretely just and merciful ways in the world?" to, "What do people who are unchurched want, and like, and how do we provide that for them so that they will join us?"

One wildly successful church, in terms of bottom-line number crunching, began with a pastor standing on a street corner ostensibly conducting a survey. He asked people what their favorite kind of music was, their preferred television shows, what kind of coffee they drank, and so on, including their favorite guilty pleasures for snacks. The surveyor/minister then formatted a church plant with a band that played Christian rock. Several Starbucks carts were deployed throughout the campus. The church even had a $30,000 Krispy Kreme donut budget. Ask what people want, build it, and they will come.

If people want upbeat, highly charged, music-infused worship experiences with celebrity ministers who resemble game show hosts and who always keep everything moving and positive, then let's do that. If people want a one-stop-shopping church where they can get their spirituality, social life around a caffeine buzz, Christian yoga and cardio-karate classes, childcare, sports leagues, as well as movie and concert nights, then why not create the Mall Church so our people can be "in the world but not of the world" but hardly notice the difference? The marketing-oriented American church is moving toward an R-21 insulated Christian ghetto sequestered away from any and every questionable influence our children could face. This brand of ecclesiology has perfected the urban flight, even baptizing it into Christ. Such separation from the world must be named for what it is:

sin, specifically the sin of abandoning our place and call to be in and for the world.

Add to these daunting barriers of resistance the tenacious American belief in rugged individualism, a fiercely guarded private life, and the notion that each individual has the personal right and privilege to the acquisition of money and property. Once acquired, each person is assumed to have personal and unaccountable sovereignty over its used and distribution. Here we have a kind of strong ideological gospel that is probably preached more consistently in our homes than any other gospel our children hear. Stepping into a pulpit to speak a word for economic justice when there is so much resistance can be a daunting prospect. So how do we do it, if we dare try? Let me suggest several possible paths through the resistance.

Negotiating Just Preaching Paths through Resistance

The Ironic Path

Garrison Keillor's story "The Prophet," which I mentioned earlier, is actually a masterful piece of prophetic discourse. Keillor sneaks his version of the prophetic truth in sideways, all the while denying that he would ever accept God's invitation to be a prophet. Purporting to deny God's prophetic call, confessing his life of lies, he disarms his hearer. Covertly and overtly, he names the truth as he sees it. Deftly using humor, he names one truth that he knew that day God called him and he refused to respond: it was the fourth of July and it was snowing. Everyone else was in denial—"It's not snow; it's just fluff from the dogwood trees!" No one around young Gary could tolerate the idea of snow in July after such a hard winter in Minnesota. But Gary knew the truth: fluff from dogwood trees does not melt on your plate while you wait in line for your hot dog. Building off that mundane truth in the face of his community's refusal to see, Keillor slips in his political critique by wondering aloud what a prophet might actually say to America. In the process, he condemns America's bullying of the world through power and prideful gloating over its military prowess. He insists that he is not a prophet, but not because he is unsure of what a prophet might say. He knows what needs to be said; he just chooses not to say it. He doesn't, after all, want to lose his invitations to his neighbor's wedding receptions. But in spite of his denials, he lays out the prophetic truth anyway. And by the time he does, his hearers, whether they agree with him or not, are all ears. An astute preacher may find the ironic path a way to get a hard word in edgewise.

The Indirect Path

Fred Craddock appealed to storytelling in his preaching as a means of "narrative indirection" in order to get a word through to those who had "heard it all before." People love a good story and Craddock capitalized on this reality by leading them down a mesmerizing route of aesthetic pleasure before then unveiling a personalized truth to a disarmed audience when they could no longer remember how to marshal a defense. Resurrecting Craddock's wise counsel on inductive preaching would be another useful strategy for preaching on justice, especially for hearers who have an allergy for imperatives, which is most of us. Storytelling that weaves plot and characters toward a gospel end of confrontation with self and God allows the preacher to become a narrative prophet in the mode of the Old Testament figure of Nathan before David in 2 Samuel 12. That story has become the prime exemplar for effective narrative indirection, but it is rarely appreciated as a story about economic injustice. Swept up in the story of an injustice done by one powerful and rich man to his poor neighbor, David was coaxed into prophetic outrage and condemnation of the powerful, rich, yet heartless man, who of course turned out to be himself in his unjust treatment of Uriah, Bathsheba, and even all Israel. The resources for storytelling in preaching are numerous, and I encourage preachers to reopen those files for use on justice matters in the pulpit.

The Path of "Soft-Sell" Justice

When I began charting the course for the book *Just Preaching: Prophetic Voices on Economic Justice*, I suspected that most people's perception of prophetic preaching was the stereotypical big and blustery, forehead-mopping oratory that puts everyone on the edge of their seat and on notice. I also assumed that most preachers feel that to preach effectively in the justice mode of discourse means looking and sounding like Martin Luther King Jr. or William Sloan Coffin. That image quickly dampens the courage of most "ordinary preachers" who might wish to wear the prophetic mantel in their local charges. My goal in *Just Preaching* was to portray a range of voices and approaches. I culled through hundreds of sermons from preachers throughout the United States seeking to find that range from, for lack of a better term, "hard-sell" to "soft-sell" approaches.

Some of the entries in *Just Preaching* are what one might expect: hard-hitting orations, chock full of facts, statistics, and white-hot passion. The contributions by James Forbes, Coffin, Marion Wright Edelman, and Walter Burghardt fit this mode. But others do not attack so much as coax. The sermons by Mary Catherine Hilkert, Pamela Couture, and Jim Burklo each give a glimpse of a kind of preaching on justice that sneaks up so slyly on hearers that they may even think they're in a feel-good sermon moment.

In Hilkert's sermon, for instance, she relates a story from Anne Lamott in which her young son accidentally became locked behind a bedroom door. The child was frightened and crying, but was too young to understand Anne's instructions on how to unlock the door. She phoned someone to come help. All she could do until the friend arrived was slide two of her fingers under the door for her son to hold onto while they both waited for deliverance and reunion. The boy calmed down and went to sleep clutching her two fingers. The force of the story encapsulates the nature of Christian faith and hope as we grasp tightly onto small mysteries God has given us, the down payments and guarantees of our ultimate deliverance. But the story also propels us to mission since any of us can be those "two fingers" by means of a phone call, a cup of coffee, or a sympathy card—simple acts of simple justice-making and keeping for people who are suffering and alone.[5]

Each of the "soft-sell" justice sermons is held together by a single, simple image that shows what justice looks like for one person at a moment in time. As a kind of pastoral justice, such sermons don't ram justice down the hearer's ear canals, nor do they try to name or solve all the world's ills in twenty minutes. And, frankly, when the only kind of justice sermons people hear are the loud and confrontational type, hearers build up a tolerance level and defense system against them, resistance hardens, and potential effectiveness wanes. To preach well and effectively on justice, one must develop a repertoire of approaches.

The Path of Scribal Traditioning

In one of *Just Preaching*'s essays, "Ancient Utterance and Contemporary Hearing," Walter Brueggemann helps preachers reimagine the preaching task from the vantage point not of the prophet but of the scribe.

5. See Hilkert, "Two Fingers under the Door," in Resner, ed., *Just Preaching*.

Brueggemann rightly notes that most preachers are probably better suited seeing themselves as descendants of the scribal corps, those trained religious leaders whose job it was to faithfully steward old texts of Scripture into their present day community's life.

Some of the texts that scribes reinscribe for the present are the prophetic writings. As a scribe, one's sole job is to faithfully bring a recognized authoritative text into the present. Expanding on Brueggemann's category, the preacher's role can be seen as a kind of dual or hybrid relation to the older text and newer context. She can and must, on the one hand, bring the content and force of the original text from the past into the community's present. In this aspect of her role, her effectiveness and faithfulness depends on accuracy and continuity. She must do what she can to make sure the old text is heard for what it was. On the other hand, the preacher as scribe stands in solidarity alongside the present-day hearers of these old textual traditions. In this role she takes her place as a fellow hearer and receiver of the prophetic tradition, a participating member of the current receiving community. To be effective in this aspect of her role, she can help facilitate the community's reception of the older textual tradition by the way that she herself models the reception. This makes the preacher-as-scribe a live interpreter, not merely a dispassionate transmitter.

Barbara Brown Taylor models the role of the hybrid scribe in her oral interpretation of the prophet Amos before her sermon "Famine in the Land."[6] After reading part of a prophetic oracle, which ought to jolt the hearers, but sensing that it may not, because hearers of Scripture readings in church are often distracted and unexpectant, she interrupts the reading with personal, interpretive commentary before returning to the reading. After another snippet of the prophet she makes a further interpretive comment before delivering the final oracle. Her own disarming and guiding comments cause the audience to be all ears to the text, which allows her to launch effectively into her sermon. Observe how she weaves back and forth in illustrating the role of the hybrid scribe:

> "The time is surely coming, says the Lord God,
> when I will send a famine on the land;
> not a famine of bread, or a thirst for water,
> but of hearing the words of the Lord." (Amos 8:11)

> I polled a lot of people this week, and Amos is no one's idea of a good time:

---

6. Taylor, "Famine," in Resner, ed., *Just Preaching*, 179–183.

Preaching Economic Justice in Lent

"Hear this, you that trample on the needy,
and bring to ruin the poor of the land." (8:4)

If you were channel-surfing on Sunday morning, would you stick around to hear the rest of that?

"On that day, says the Lord God,
I will make the sun go down at noon,
and darken the earth in broad daylight.
I will turn your feasts into mourning,
and all your songs into lamentation;
I will bring sackcloth on all loins,
and baldness on every head;
I will make it like the mourning for an only son,
and the end of it like a bitter day." (8:9–10)

Why is Amos in such a bad mood? Because . . .

The preacher who follows the path of scribal traditioning extends Karl Barth's helpful description of the preacher's primary role as the bearer of Scripture's words: "We bear witness to that [the biblical] witness."[7] Brueggemann, Barth, and Taylor all remind us that even though we may not fancy ourselves as stereotypical social justice–type preachers, if the texts that the tradition hands down to us are justice-prone and, on analysis, pertinent to our situations, we have both a responsibility as well as an alternate strategy to pass them along faithfully and effectively.

Faithful traditioning of these biblical calls to justice requires that we render such claims in homiletically authentic and consistent ways. This means doing what Thomas G. Long insists is the key to being biblical in our preaching: saying and doing in our sermons what the biblical writers were saying and doing in their texts.[8] As Long helpfully instructs, this does not mean that preachers must say what the biblical writers said in the way that they said it. Preaching on a proverb does not mean the sermon has to take the form of a proverb. Preaching on a psalm does not require a poem-like sermon. And preaching from the prophets does not require the preacher putting on Elijah's mantle and ranting and raving. It doesn't require preaching naked, angrily, or violently. The form and style will depend more on the current preacher and context. Witness Barbara Brown Taylor's own personality setting the tone for her use of Amos. Like Keillor, a sermon on

---

7. Barth, *Homiletics*, 22.
8. Long, *Witness*, ch. 4.

hard prophetic truth can take the ironic form of a confessed lie and denial of God's call. Like Craddock (and Nathan), a prophetic sermon may coax hearers to the truth through a sneaky narrative that sets them up for the punch line.

The Preacher as Importunate Widow and Kierkegaardian Clown

Why do people change? It is a hotly debated subject, but I have become convinced that the number-one reason people are motivated to life-altering change is due to some traumatic event, some crisis, some significant loss.[9] If I am correct, then a key problem in attempting to promote social and economic justice in our preaching is this: preaching can announce the crisis of our world and God's own outrage at the crisis. Preaching can announce the crucifixion and resurrection of Jesus as a response of God to our world's injustice and God's desire to rectify it. Preaching can even announce God's call to us to be stewards and agents of God's own desire for justice and shalom in this world. But how do these preached words about crisis take existential hold of our hearers such that they effect life and world-transforming change? Only life-altering experiences compel at-any-cost modification of one's existence so that a person engages in true accompaniment of this world's vulnerable and stubborn advocacy for this world's damned ones. There would be no Amber Alert had there not been the tragic abduction and murder of nine-year-old Amber Hagerman in Arlington, Texas in 1996. There would be no Mothers Against Drunk Drivers (MADD) had thirteen-year-old Cari Lightner not been killed by a hit-and-run drunk driver in Fair Oaks, California, in 1980.

The homiletical question behind preaching on justice that wishes to be effective in motivating those who hear to lives that reflect God's desire

---

9. Change theorist Jeffrey A. Kottler essentially concurs with my own conviction: "Although a small minority of people might mention something that happened in therapy, or a classroom, or formal learning experience, the vast majority of cases [of change] occurred after recovering from a challenging or even traumatic event—the death of a loved one, a major failure or disappointment, a crisis or catastrophe, a relationship or job ending, a threatening illness, or something similar. We know now from research on this topic that traumatic or difficult events don't necessarily lead to incapacitating problems but also can spark tremendous growth and learning. In fact, they do so just as often as they may lead to trauma." Kottler, "What REALLY Leads to Change."

Preaching Economic Justice in Lent

for justice is this: where is the trauma, the crisis, that compels us to act, not out of guilt or fear, but because we are convicted that there is no other reason for us to be alive other than to see love and justice—God's true shalom—sweep over the earth and pervade every human, social, political, and economic relationship?

The methods and strategies discussed above—the paths of irony, indirection, and scribal traditioning—all point to means by which sermons might illicit heightened awareness, and even possible incremental change. These strategies would hopefully increase the frequency of our preaching on justice, and maybe even its effectiveness. But a hard truth remains: if crisis is the key to substantive and systemic change, are we as preachers ultimately doomed in our prophetic calls to economic justice? How, indeed, can the need for justice become transformationally apparent and existentially non-negotiable? How does justice become as essential for the church's life as the air that it breathes?

Maybe these questions lead us to a logical cul-de-sac. To preach on the topic of economic justice in the North American pulpit may be similar to a clown trying to be serious. Soren Kierkegaard, the nineteenth-century Danish philosopher and theologian, found himself in a situation similar to us today. It takes no interpretive leap to feel Kierkegaard's frustration with the lethargic church of his day. In his frustration he turned to parables to attempt to thaw the frozen consciousness of a hardened church mind and life. One parable tells of an audience gathered at a theatre for an evening play. A fire erupts backstage. One of the actors, dressed as a clown, runs onto the stage and yells, "Fire! Fire!" Assuming this is part of the play, the people laugh, commenting on how impressive the clown's acting skills are. No matter how much the clown protests, states the "God's honest truth," and punctuates his cries with tone or gestures, the people only applaud and enjoy the performance as an act of entertainment. If it were not for the reality of the fire, they would presumably go about their lives after the show pretty much the same as they had before the performance. That seems to be the case with most sermons.[10]

Why do we preachers not just give up? Is it possible to confess and repent of our timidity? Is it possible for us to trust in the preached word's efficacy when we see and experience so much of our calls for justice going unheeded? Does this explain why preachers tend to focus much of their

---

10. See Kierkegaard, *Parables*, 3. I have expanded on his parable for my purposes here.

preaching on changing people's thinking rather than their acting—because it is much more difficult to assess success and failure on something that is less visibly measurable?

As a way of concluding, I wish to suggest one more image for preachers to reflect upon in their attempts to stay the course in sounding forth God's desire for justice in a world seemingly bent on avoiding it. The image is from Luke 18, the story about the persistent widow and the unjust judge.

She has been called "the importunate widow." The adjective describes her as persistent, but the word also suggests a persistence that veers into the realm of the annoying, the demanding, the doggedly insistent. I'm not suggesting that preachers be so obvious as to be unnecessarily annoying in their persistent call for justice. Indeed, the suggested paths above—the ironic, the indirect, the soft-sell, and the scribal—attempt to help preachers come at justice from such different angles that hearers will not weary of the sermonic assault. I like this image in spite of its potential negative undertones because it portrays an image of a determined and tenacious voice and presence that takes the cry for justice personally. The hearers in this scenario are identified with the unjust judge, someone that the text describes as neither fearing God nor respecting any human being. This is admittedly a rather unkind portrait of the congregation, but in matters of justice, especially economic justice, the description may be frighteningly fitting. The tight-fisted greediness of especially wealthy white congregations in North America has led to a virtual gag order on justice sermons in the tall-steeple-downtown churches. But in spite of overwhelming odds, the widow did not back down and she did not shut up. Though the unjust, non-heeding judge had no reason to do anything that she asked, she persisted. Finally, he relented.

The widow here illustrates what Charles Campbell has argued is preaching's ethic: preaching is itself an act of doing justice against the powers and principalities of this world that stand opposed to God's ways and will.[11] Preaching is no mere cheap talk. To preach the gospel is to do the gospel. To preach justice is the do justice. Preaching justice begins the process of effecting justice in the lives of people, who, by the miracle of God's gift and grace, do hear and are transformed. In spite of the enormity of preacher and hearing failings, preaching justice does raise awareness, motivate concrete acts of accompaniment with the disadvantaged, and spur advocacy for change of unjust systems.

---

11. Campbell, *Word Before the Powers*.

Preaching Economic Justice in Lent

The just preacher who takes on the role of the importunate widow is the opposite of the defeatist attitude canonized in Murphy's Law when it comes to praying the Lord's Prayer. Murphy—he of the law that expects the worst, who assumes fatalistically that "what can happen will happen"—is turned inside out and upside down by the just preacher as stubbornly persistent widow. Because she insists, over and over, that "what *will* happen *can* happen." This is to bring an eschatological dimension to one's prayers, pleas, and sermons of protest. Jesus taught us to pray, "Thy will be done on earth as it is in heaven." The persevering widow-preacher is curious about the last part of that petition: "What does God *will*? What happens in *heaven*?" She asks that because, believing Jesus' prayer to be the right prayer, she is then more emboldened: "*Whatever God wills, whatever happens in heaven, by God, must happen here, on earth!*"

The church exists to continue the eschatological reversal of Murphy's Law in this world, and especially for those in this world who have known nothing else than the worst this world has to offer. If in God's heaven the lonely are and will be enveloped in loving and supportive community, then what will happen can happen. The church can be that safe, loving, and supportive community now. If in God's heaven the hungry are filled, then what will happen can happen. The church can become the community of the welcoming table to feed the hungry. If in God's heaven the naked are clothed, the sick are healed, and the widows, orphans, and strangers are cared for and given family, then what will happen can happen. The church can become that hundredfold family of blessing that Jesus promised (Mark 10:30).

Preachers must not be naively optimistic, nor should we be given over to despair or cynicism. Rather, we are the spokespersons for a tenaciously eschatological people: what will happen can happen, and by God, for God, and because of God's own covenant faithfulness=tenaciousness, these Kingdom things must happen in and through our words and actions. In fact, our baptism guarantees it. For baptism itself is the trauma and crisis—death, burial, and resurrection—that we all need to transform our lives from complacency to obsessive drivenness for justice. Our existential crisis is real: we have died and been raised again by God's grace. From that grave we have been raised to be a new creation, and part of God's long anticipated New Creation, the world of God's shalom, mercy, and justice.

7

Preaching the Cross:
A Confessional Pilgrimage

Introduction

SEVERAL YEARS AGO I was "talking preaching" with a man who was the first significantly different voice I heard from the pulpit in my teens and early twenties. I don't remember how we got around to the question, but at one point he asked me, "What is preaching's message?" I answered quickly, "The cross." Not wanting an answer to his next question, he curtly asked, "What does *that* mean?"

His concern, with sensitivities nurtured by Tillich, was the meaning, or lack thereof, that "the cross" has to hearers. My initial, though unspoken response, nurtured by Barthian impulses, was, "If the cross's significance consists in what God does apart from human initiative or understanding, what does 'meaning' matter?" Beneath both our theological inclinations, though, was the fear that "the word of the cross" had become a mere code word for insiders, and as such was as meaningless to us as it was to anyone else, not withstanding Barth's point.

Using the right code words within a particular community's own language game can be reassuring to those inside. But such words and phrases can be nothing more than comfort words, words that make insiders feel safe. Comfort words are those that have lost both their referential character and their point of contact with hearers not familiar with the game we are playing. As such, they function in a purely intramural way within the community. "The word of the cross" is such a word. Like Woody Allen's chameleon character, Leonard Zelig, the word of the cross has morphed into the shape, size, color, and accent of various groups throughout time. Such morphing has not always led to comfort.

Preaching the Cross: A Confessional Pilgrimage

The First Naïveté

I grew up in an iconoclastic church. Great care was taken to insure that the worship space was void of any religious symbols. That meant no crosses, no stained glass, no saints, no banners, no vestments or colors—nothing that might misguide the imagination into idolatry. Of course, my ecclesiastical interior designers did not take into account that the human imagination cannot *not* produce images. So, by default, my imagination had what appeared to be a blank canvas upon which to paint. But I say "appeared to be" because the canvas was still there, as were the tubes of paint and the brushes. All the art supplies were in stock. The icons of religious symbolism that were trying hard not to be such took on great power in their denial.

I remember in the church of my youth a spare pulpit that was oak with a light stain and a glossy finish. A microphone jutted out of the middle and back to the mouth of the preacher. It was up four steps and to the left side, in balance with a reading lectern on the right. Such a declaration of space required the preacher—always a man—to stand and speak continuously for thirty to forty-five minutes while the congregation sat still and quiet in long, thinly cushioned oak pews. The situation looked strikingly similar to the authoritarian situation of discipline ("lecturing") in many people's social framework, where those who were "in trouble" because of wrongdoing would sit erect and silent on the couch while their father would stand, sometimes pacing back and forth, and mete out correction mingled with disappointment.

Between the pulpit and lectern, but several steps down, yet one step up from the congregation, was a rectangular table upon which sat unadorned but shiny silver trays. Etched across the top front edge of the table were the words "Do this in remembrance of me." Within the smaller trays, my mind's eye could see the saltless saltine crackers lying on a doily in the dark, passively awaiting the lifting of the lid on Sunday morning. Under the lids of the larger trays were the tiny shot glasses filled three fourths of the way up with Welch's grape juice. Just looking at the trays and the words across the top front edge of the table made me remember the words frequently spoken before Communion. In good Zwinglian fashion we were reminded every week that the "bread" and "fruit of the vine" were mere symbols and not really the body and blood of Christ. Funny, but the more the men pleaded this way, the more a voice whispered in my ear, "Methinks thou protesteth a bit too strongly" (we used the King James Version).

PART 2—PROCLAIMING GOD'S REIGN IN A WORLD THAT IS PASSING AWAY

In every church of my childhood there was a baptistry in a prominent place. It symbolized the place of new beginning, of salvation, of the cleansing of sin by the blood of the Lamb. Since the churches I grew up in practiced immersion of adults, the baptistry was always the largest entity up front, a fact that spoke of its importance to the proceedings. Indeed, virtually every word from the pulpit culminated in a call to be baptized into Christ, even if everyone there had already been immersed, and immersed "correctly." And that's the other thing the baptistry symbolized for me: correct religion. We had baptism right. Other churches had it wrong. The right/wrong, correct/incorrect, true teachers/false teachers, orthodox/heretical mentality pervaded everything seen, said, and heard in the worship space. It created a deep sense of fear and uncertainty, but also a warm, safe feeling for the guardians of the code.

Though no crosses adorned the churches in which I grew up, either inside or outside, I remember hearing about the cross every Sunday. The word of the cross in my church family of origin was a word about sin and the way our sin separated us from the holy God. Jesus' sacrifice on the cross was God's way of providing the necessary payment for our reconciliation, redemption, and salvation. Without Jesus' death on the cross we would remain lost in our sins. The word of the cross was summarized in the song, "He paid a debt he did not owe. I owed a debt I could not pay. I needed someone to wash my sins away. And now I sing a brand new song, 'Amazing Grace.' Christ Jesus paid the debt that I could never pay." The word of the cross was spoken exclusively in the language of substitutionary atonement and was focused on the individual. My church of origin was a white, conservative, middle-class church of the conservative South. Racism, misogyny, and classism bubbled beneath, if not directly on top of the surface, though I grew up virtually blind to these realities since such sentiments came out of some of the same mouths as those who spoke of God and the cross to me.

I had no operative hermeneutic of suspicion growing up, but do remember nascent questions that lurked, questions such as, "If God is really God, then why is the Divine confined within the sacrificial system? Where did that system come from anyway? How does the shedding of blood atone for sin?" It seemed simplistic and formulaic. The justification for it was confined to texts of Scripture from Paul and Hebrews, with some Old Testament texts on sacrifice amended for support. I remember being puzzled by the Gospels' conspicuous and almost total silence about atonement matters. My ministers and teachers at the time told me that the gospel stories were best explained by the epistles. That is why the preaching I heard was based more in the epistles, and was primarily didactic in character. The point of contact (*anknupfungspunkt*) for people with the word of the cross had purely to do with their own recognition of personal sin, desire for forgiveness, repentance, and submission to baptism, in which Christ's blood proved efficacious for their sins' removal. Evangelism and preaching took the route of "pricking the conscience," or at least achieving an intellectual assent to the idea that without the cross, without Christ's sacrificially shed blood, and without our coming in contact with that in baptism by immersion, we would go to hell.

The Critical Period

I succeeded as an evangelist of the traditional gospel of the cross—a gospel that focused on the personal and private but avoided the public and the social—but cracks in the earthen vessel were starting to show. In one evangelistic encounter, I remember convincing (at least cognitively) one woman of her sin and her need for Christ's sacrificial atonement, which she could only access by obedience to the waters of baptism. She was persuaded, but reluctantly. I'll never forget her words: "This seems right, but something about it smells fishy."

Soon I found myself at a Christian university and introduced for the first time to the critical study of the Bible, history, and theology. Though the effect on my childhood faith was about a 9.5 on the Richter scale (my alma mater sat on top of the San Andreas fault), I recognized only later that the ark of my understanding of the word of the cross remained relatively untouched. Even so, this period brought two significant alterations to the simple formula.

The first was the important new awareness, gained primarily from Paul, that sin was not merely to be understood as discreet acts of moral rebellion on our part, one of which was potent enough to knock us off the tightrope of faith, below which no safety net lay. Sin, rather, was a realm of power in which we were inexorably stuck. God's graceful gift in Christ's death on the cross was a miraculous deliverance from sin's realm that transports us into Christ. The second, also from Paul, was the related realization that salvation was not merely individualistic. Paul's pronouns are persistently plural. There are no "Lone Ranger" Christians, as my old New

Testament professor liked to say. The "in Christ" realm is profoundly communal. The cross as the gift of God's grace thus became for me a point of solidarity with all whom God called, judged, redeemed, and initiated into the household of faith.

The deeper and more disturbing critical period of re-evaluation of the word of the cross did not really begin, I am not proud to confess, until my doctoral work. There I was introduced to the perspectives of non-white, non-European, non-male readers and hearers of the word of the cross. My immediate response to these "other" readings and hearings was reactionary. My way of reading Scripture and hearing the word of the cross was not merely *a* way of reading and hearing; it was *the* way. I had been taught that if we all signed on to the same neutral, best methods of research (mainly, the historical and traditional literary-critical methods), we would all end up in the same place. Unaware of my own social location, and the way that the forebears of my social location had both produced these particular methods and then wielded them with hegemonic power over all theological realms, I found myself on a steep and threatening learning curve. Discovering who I was, where these ostensibly neutral methods had come from, and how they had been used to keep control of those unlike us, I learned that my social location and its servant methods postured me to read and hear what I read and heard. I learned that my facility to dispatch what I saw as hermeneutically ill-conceived specks in other people's eyes (with the same kind of speed and vigor that I had evangelized those not-baptized-correctly folks in my youth) was due to the hegemonic beam in my own eye. Even in my dissertation, a treatise on the message of the cross and its importance for the person of the preacher, I proved myself a good imitator of Job's friends by dismissing virtually without sympathy the experience of someone for whom the word of the cross has been nothing but bad news, brutality, and the antithesis of love and redemption. I now find my words in that dissertation to be too quick, too sure, and not too full of the grace that is a crucial aspect of the word of the cross.

The critical period threatens to undo everything that came before in one's world of faith. It is a fire that relentlessly burns everything in its path. When one suffers through the sifting, the burning, the shaking of the foundations, one wonders what, if anything, will remain. Of necessity, for a time everything does seem lost. The center of one's being no longer holds. It is wilderness and wandering, waterless clouds and dried-up brooks. It is that downtime that Qoheleth warned us about on the negative side of each

Preaching the Cross: A Confessional Pilgrimage

antithesis, the time of death, uprooting, killing, tearing down, weeping, non-embrace, mourning, losing, casting away, rending, hating, war. It is, for the preacher, the profoundly threatening time to keep silence. We want to retreat back to a simpler time, but know that there is no going back. Paul Ricoeur comments on this experience: "Does that mean that we could go back to a primitive naïveté? Not at all. In every way, something has been lost, irremediably lost: immediacy of belief. But if we can no longer live the great symbolisms of the sacred in accordance with the original belief in them, we can, we modern men [and women], aim at a second naïveté in and through criticism."[1]

As I travelled through the critical period, I learned that folks from my social location have had the audacity to take a God's-eye point of view regarding the cross and have forced that view on everyone else as the normative and, often, as the only view.

As I look back, I see that the seeds for my critical period were planted long ago by several key experiences. My first consciousness-altering experience with the cross occurred when I saw in a history book a black and white photograph that had at its center a burning cross on the front lawn of a house. Between the house and the cross, a black man was hanging at the end of a rope. On the far left sat men on horseback wearing a white robe and hood. I could not reconcile what I knew of God, of Christ, of the gospel, and of the cross with this gross act of hatred and violence. The second experience occurred in a church history class when I read how the converted emperor Constantine had ordered that the cross be carried first into battle. Eusebius of Caesarea tells us that Constantine had a vision wherein he saw the trophy of a cross of light in the heavens, with the inscription "CONQUER BY THIS." Constantine was unsure of its meaning, but then Jesus himself appeared to Constantine and told him to use it as a safeguard against all his enemies.[2] Crusaders wore the cross stitched on their chests as they slaughtered Jews and Muslims on their rapacious path to free Jerusalem, in a stunningly different sense than the cross first freed Jerusalem. It crossed my mind that evangelism would be quite effective if done on a horse with a sword drawn in one hand and the words of invitation to the infidels "Be baptized or die!" on our lips. Just what sort of converts one would end up with is quite another story. Though less physically violent,

---

1. Ricoeur, *Symbolism*, 351.
2. Eusebius, *Life of Constantine*, bk. 1, chs. 28–29.

this had been my method of evangelism too—the kind that made that one woman smell fish.

The experience of feeling the horror of this use of the cross came back to me one evening while I sat in a seminary chapel waiting for a worship service to begin. Lifting up my eyes from the printed order on my lap, I beheld a massive twenty-foot polished steel sword attached to a cutting board hanging from the wall in the chapel. My first thought was, "What is *that* doing in here?" It was a true Wittgensteinian duck/rabbit moment. Then the duck became a rabbit and I saw that it was actually a cross suspended on a wooden backdrop. I breathed a sigh of relief that I hadn't actually asked my question out loud. Given Wittgenstein's idea of exclusion, however, the implications of my chapel experience for preaching are profound. Applied to my "It's a sword, no, it's a cross!" situation, the thing itself cannot be both at once. The vision of one excludes the other. And there can be no middle ground, no cross/sword entity simultaneously. Those for whom the cross has had only a sword function in their mental and physical experience can only see a sword, no matter how loudly the preacher preaches, unless they—by the grace of God—undergo a radical perceptual and experiential paradigm shift for the cross to become a redemptive image of love, and show the sword the door.

Getting in touch with my own ethnic, racial, and religious roots has sensitized me to the brutal forces that the Jews—my relatives—have experienced, often at the hands of Christians who held the cross as a sword in their own way. From Melito of Sardis to the Holocaust, Christians have justified anti-Semitism on the basis that the Jews were Christ-killers and thus God-murderers. Throughout the Jews' experience, the cross has been used against them by Christians, as a tool of violence. Naftali Lavie poignantly describes her experience of the cross as symbol of hate:

> Last month I stood with my immediate family—my wife, my daughter and my three sons at the Block of Horrors in Auschwitz. . . . From a window on the second floor, a huge wooden cross, eight metres high, blocked my view. Behind it stood the Carmelite convent. . . . Many Jews see the presence of the cross at Auschwitz as a provocation directed at the Jewish people, and as a desecration of the Holocaust. . . . I still remembered the fears that haunted us as children in Poland, as we tried to escape the presence of the cross. In our heavily Christian communities, Catholic funeral processions were always led by a young boy holding a long metal scepter with a cross on top. Behind the child the priest would

march, reading the prayers. Any Christian passerby meeting the procession would remove his hat, bend his knee and bow to the cross. Jewish adults knew how to handle this situation, sometimes seeking shelter in doorways to avoid confronting the cross. Children were less experienced, and were occasionally beaten when the procession passed by and they did not bend their knee before the cross. . . . Those who raised the cross in Auschwitz perhaps meant to erase the uniqueness of what happened to the Jews in this evil place. But by doing this they have returned the symbol that has pursued us down through the generations to its proper place. There within eyesight of the gallows on which the commandant of Auschwitz was hanged, stands the cross—fitting reminder to the world of who is responsible for the most horrible crime since the beginning of time.[3]

I am quite sure that the Carmelites meant no harm. I would guess they were only trying to gather up all the senseless suffering at Auschwitz in the only symbol they knew to be large enough to do so. But the question "What does that mean?" would have been a good question to ask the Jewish observers before the cross was imposed on their visual landscape.

The conquest of the Americas by European settlers continued the cross's violent thrust into the belly of weaker people by those who came to dominate and own, even while they evangelized along the way. Slave peoples from Africa, women from every human sector, and native people in the lands of colonization have all endured disgusting renditions of the cross. It is enough to make us ask with absolute seriousness the question that Mary C. Boys asked several years ago: "Is the cross a symbol Christians should now lay aside?"[4]

The Second Naïveté

Reading eighteenth- and nineteenth-century homiletical literature, I came across a prophetic printing error: "The Rise of Scared Rhetoric." The author meant "sacred rhetoric," of course, but the typesetter, perhaps subconsciously, anticipated the fear that Barth meant to put into the heart of rhetoric-heavy homiletic approaches. It worked that way for me. Reading Barth's *Word of God and Word of Man* in 1980, I never wanted to preach again. Barth's warning descended "from above" in the question, "Who are

3. Naftali Lavie, "Cross and Gallows," quoted in Boys, "Cross," 17.
4. Boys, "Cross."

you, O mortal, with the word of God on your lips?" My answer: "I'm nobody, nothing; I give up!"

The new cause for pause in this preacher ascended "from below": "Who are you, O white, middle-class, heterosexual male to speak a word of suffering, a word of the cross, to us whose existence has been virtually nothing but suffering and cruciform?" Reflecting on this to near paralysis, I have seriously wondered how I could continue to hold onto an instrument of death that killed not the sin but the sinner again and again.

Paul Ricoeur insists that there exists the promise of breaking through and getting beyond the critical period—that period in which all is questioned and much is lost—to a new arena in which one is able even to claim enduring old truths and convictions from the land of the first naïveté, even though one now "knows better." Ricoeur's is a word of hermeneutical gospel, almost too good to be true. Arrival at such a place is a great and surprising gift. I do not feel that I have fully emerged from my current critical period of examining the word of the cross. I doubt that one ever can on the matter of the cross. As Ricoeur shows, the hermeneutical process of understanding is not a one-time, linear, sequential phenomenon. The sequence of first naïveté, critical period, and second naïveté is heuristic and flexible.

What It Might Mean to Preach the Cross Today

As I currently read the literature of Hispanic and Latino theology and edit a book on behalf of the National Interfaith Hospitality Network on issues of poverty, homelessness, and socially conscious preaching, I find myself straddling the border of the critical period and the second naïveté. Not attempting to be exhaustive, what follows are three suggestions regarding "preaching the cross" in light of the current theological and social situations in especially North American Christian contexts.

> *1. Preaching the cross means to resist triumphalism and glory and to risk folly and absurdity: in a word, to preach the cross today means to participate in the Spirit's groaning toward redemption.*

This may be a nearly impossible task, especially in those North American churches that are getting the most press because they are experiencing the most "success." Paul was the first we know of to speak of the complete absurdity of the cross's message. The message of the cross strained the bounds of morality, decency, and intelligence for both Jews and Gentiles. Paul's irony and sarcasm are thick as he describes not only the message but also the nature of its preaching and ministry. I cannot imagine the apostle meaning that the cross's absurdity had an expiration date on it—say, until Constantine became a Christian, or America turned Christianity into big business and the cross into a pop-fashion bauble. The contemporary scandal of the cross is one that Mary Catherine Hilkert has named well: "In Christian faith the last word about the cross may be that it is indeed a mystery of divine love, fidelity, and solidarity, but in the context of global suffering the first word that must be spoken is of its scandal, injustice, and absurdity."[5] The absurdity exists partly in this: the cross is a sign of humanity's rejection of God's version of God's self. If T. S. Eliot was right in saying, "Humankind cannot take too much reality," it is doubly correct to say that what we see in the incarnation of God in Jesus is that humankind cannot take too much of God. Humankind witnessed God's version of God and said, "No thank you. We'd rather not." It was indeed foolhardy of God to attempt to come among us and embody love. It was a waste of God-time (*kairos*) to spend a life up close and personal with humankind when all we did was spit it back in God's face in the end. The rejection of God's self and God's taking our rejection in humiliation is cause for outcry. The death of God, for pure love and forgiveness, is cause for lament. Every time God's image is spit back again at God, lament is the only appropriate language of response.

In a culture that thrives in the denial of death, the church flees the tomb in search of a risen Lord too quickly. Good Friday must be given its say. Lament is an appropriate form for the cross to be preached today. Jesus' own words from the cross were few and brief, but Matthew and Mark tell us they included lament in good psalmic fashion: "My God, my God, why have you abandoned me?" Lament as a mode for preaching the cross today sees part of preaching's task as one wherein the real questions and absurdities of people's lives are gathered up and given voice in the pulpit, in worship, and in the presence of the community of faith. Preaching the cross today sees the places where love has been abandoned and asks, "Why, O Lord, must these children be left alone, be raised by only one parent, be abandoned on the street to fend for themselves? And, how long before they know the safety and warmth of an embrace that does not hide motivations

---

5. Hilkert, "Preaching the Folly of the Cross."

for abuse and violence? How long before they know the face of pure, non-violating, non-manipulative love?"

Preaching the cross means articulating the questions for today's sufferers, questions they may not know how to ask for themselves, questions they may not feel free to ask in the context of worship and in the context of the worshipping community of faith—in the face of God. Churches for whom worship has devolved into mere celebration cannot even imagine how questions and outcries could have a legitimate part of the program. Church music that has devolved into only "praise music" cannot imagine a place for the sons of Korah, those lament psalm specialists, to lead worship on Sunday mornings. To mirror the biblical tradition, for every praise team in our worship staff, there ought to be a lament team.

Lament as a form of preaching the cross stands on the side of the victimized and gives voice to those who suffer. Giving voice to sufferers is an act of good news. Preaching the cross means proclaiming God's involvement with us in our groaning. Groaning is one of the ways the Holy Spirit works within believers while we, along with all creation, await adoption and the redemption of our bodies (Rom 8:22–23). Adoption and redemption as hope is a confession that we have not as yet experienced the fullness of what the gospel promises. As George Steiner has suggested, we exist not on Easter Sunday nor on Good Friday, but on Saturday, the day between Jesus' death and his resurrection: a place between the reality of the cross, and all the suffering and hopelessness that the cross embraces, and the resurrection, with all the hope, resolution, reunion, and rest that it promises. In this in-between-time place we are not alone. Preaching the cross is an extension of the claim that God is with us—Emmanuel. Just as Matthew frames his entire Gospel ("they shall call him Emmanuel," 1:23; and "Lo, I am with you . . . ," 28:20) with this claim, preaching the cross continues to extend the claim of God's presence in the midst of the world's affliction, not apart from it.

This word of God's solidarity with sufferers, though, cannot be a ploy by the powerful to justify or glorify the suffering of those for whom it is in the best interests of the powerful to keep subjugated. The word of the cross that speaks of divine accompaniment in suffering rings true only when spoken by those who embody the word of accompaniment in suffering. This is not to say that the efficacy of the word preached depends on the preacher's capacity to live it out faithfully. I am not trotting out a contemporary homiletical Donatism. God, in God's mysterious grace, has caused the word of

Preaching the Cross: A Confessional Pilgrimage

the cross to become gospel even when spoken by the most corrupt personal advancement. But from the vantage point of the hearers, the word does ring hollow when it is a word that smacks of manipulation rather than true accompaniment.

Dominican missionary priest Brian Pierce experienced what true accompaniment means in Lima, Peru. On Good Friday, as he held the cross, hundreds streamed before him to kiss the feet of the crucified. However, on Easter Sunday only a smattering of people showed up to celebrate the resurrection. Disturbed by this at first, he soon realized that "there was no contradiction between the bloodied statue of Jesus in the church and faith in the Resurrection. . . . The resurrection is experienced not as final victory, but in the recognition of the close presence of the living God who chooses to walk with and suffer alongside the poor. Resurrection is joyful and faithful reassurance here and now."[6] God-with-us in suffering is resurrection hope. In the process of this kind of concrete accompaniment, sufferers experience the hope and power of resurrection, but not apart from it. Cross and resurrection proclaimed from above, without compassionate accompaniment, is simply the newest form of being stoned from the pulpit, of the hearers becoming Craddock's proverbial "javelin catchers."

Moreover, the word of the cross as the word of God's accompaniment with the sufferer is not a claim that human suffering is the will of God. The Spirit groans within creatures and creation for ultimate redemption. Christ's death and resurrection were for the ultimate making whole of all that is. Following Edward Schillebeeckx, it is truer to say that God saves in spite of the cross than because of it.[7] God uses even our means of rejecting God as a means for reclaiming us.

2. Preaching the cross is an apocalyptic act, revealing in the preacher's words and body the advent of the New Age.

The Second Helvetic Confession states that "the preaching of the word of God is the word of God." That is a bold claim. I venture a similar claim here: the preaching of the apocalypse of God is the apocalypse of God. That apocalypse is shrouded, of course, in the frailty and fallibility of human words and the humans themselves that make up the preaching moment,

---

6. Brian J. Pierce, "Cross and the Crib," quoted in Goizuez, *Caminemo con Jesús*, 210–11, n. 58.

7. See Hilkert, *Naming Grace*, 115–20.

both preachers and hearers. It is scandalously instantiated in the historical situatedness of the humans involved, thus always in danger of being reduced to the linguistic, theological, and even philosophical constraints and restrictions of those involved in its exchange. Even so, the Christian confession is that the preached word is an act of disclosure by the power of the Holy Spirit. God's great risk in preaching is to elongate what God began in the gospel's disclosure at the crucifixion and resurrection of Jesus through the speaking of preachers and the hearing of listeners. And in so doing God condescends to grasp humanity and the created order anew with a vision for what God has done, is doing, and will yet do in the consummation.

Preaching the cross is thus part of God's great reclamation project. If Jesus' death and resurrection began God's repossession of creation, preaching continues it until the final trumpet blows and every knee bows. Preaching the cross thus participates in Jesus' own death. As such it participates in the death of the old order of things and in Jesus' binding of the strong man. Preaching the cross also participates in Jesus' resurrection, and as such in God's restoration of all things.

As an act of apocalypse itself—the revelation of God and God's rectifying acts—preaching must always lead with the decisive takeover of an embattled creation by a God who will not allow God's creation to go to hell in a handbasket. Preaching thus projects God's Reign, God's Kingdom, God's will and way exacted and performed in Jesus life, death, resurrection, and promised return. The mission and ethic of the church extend out of these prior facts and realities and are an extension of them in the church's life. For the church is the body of Christ now in the world, animated by God's Spirit to: 1) continue the work that Jesus began in proclaiming the Kingdom of God and freeing people from Satan's domination, and 2) foreshadow the heavenly realm that is the ultimate fate of creation. Preaching God's apocalypse is thus an announcement of what God has done, as well as a propulsion of the faith community into a life in a broken world that brings the smell of life and hope through longsuffering acts of love and justice.

3. Preaching the cross is an act of repentance, humility, and silent solidarity with all those who suffer and are afflicted.

Having just claimed a revelatory function for the proclaimed word, I quickly add that the apocalyptic gospel must not be spoken too quickly, too glibly, and in certain contexts should be spoken only in nonverbal ways. As preachers,

Preaching the Cross: A Confessional Pilgrimage

we do not control revelation. We may not use it for our ends. We are stewards of its mystery, servants of its weakness—of its weak but strong one, Jesus Christ. In light of the world in which we live, and the lives of those to whom we are called to be stewards of the mystery and servants of the gospel, to preach it truly may mean to do so in ways that require silence first.

In his brief but still durable "orientation to theological study," Charles Wood made the disorienting suggestion that simply to say what the New Testament writers said is not necessarily to say what they said. To say what they said, in fact, may necessitate saying exactly the opposite. "Sometimes you can't say the same thing by saying the same thing; in order to say the same thing, you must say something different."[8] For those to whom this suggestion causes significant anxiety, it is helpful to remember that Jesus' unusual birth, person, teaching, death on the cross, and resurrection from the dead were all instances of God saying and doing a different thing than people had heard before, in order for God to say what God had always said about covenant faithfulness, justice, righteousness, love, and mercy.

Applied to the preaching of the cross, Wood's remarks have at least two implications:

First, to preach the cross today as they preached the cross then may mean to preach an anti-cross. In other words, preachers must take seriously the ways in which people have been afflicted by means of the cross, kept down by a dominant culture that used God, Christ, and the cross to do so. The anti-cross gospel is a word of the cross today that functions in the same subverting way as the original word of the cross. Such a word is a cry of repentance and humility. It does not exert power and glorify suffering, but cries the bitter cry of anguish for the cross's implication in deepened suffering. The anti-cross gospel is a gospel word on behalf of every African who had the cross branded into his skin while in transit to a life of hell in exile from his home and family. It is a gospel word on behalf of every Jew who was beaten for not genuflecting correctly. It is a gospel word on behalf of every woman who was beaten into submission by a man who used Christianity as a means of manipulating power over her.

Second, to preach the cross today as they preached it then may require the complete absence of words. This is not only to do the exact opposite of the apostles in Acts, but it is to reclaim the initial word of the cross in a profound sense. For, if we want to push things, the original word of the cross came as person, presence, and action. The Word did not come as a

---

8. Wood, *Vision and Discernment*, 40.

pretty or persuasive sermon in a recognizable rhetorical package of the day. He was rather the ghostly and mysterious figure of Isaiah 53 whose mouth was silent even as he came on our behalf and took on our failings on our behalf. Preachers of the cross must discern the times and places to remain silent, in order to proclaim most effectively the enigmatic word of the cross. The preaching of the cross in silence means to enter into the ministries of redemption in the form of accompaniment and advocacy among "the least of these" who are all around us. Living the cross for others is a way of preaching the cross. Putting on a tool belt at Habitat for Humanity for a day of bruising one's fingers, and building another's safe place. Taking the overnight shift at the local Interfaith Hospitality Network. Arranging for a hernia surgery for an impoverished migrant camp worker who has neither the means nor the connections to do so. Collecting and delivering heavy coats to those without cold weather gear in the inner city as winter threatens. Sitting with the lonely elderly. Playing basketball with the neglected young. Being a reliable person to those who have never known such a person. Being faithful to your spouse. Showing your own children your tender, vulnerable core of love. If what we have learned most purely in Christ's self-giving sacrifice on the cross is a love that knows no bounds, then our acceptance of that love empowers us to embody it and extend it to others in his name, especially to those nearest to us.

Wood's words are haunting: to say the same thing that they said may require that we say a different thing. There is a time to speak of the cross and a time to keep silence. Wisdom consists in knowing what time it is. Wisdom consists in understanding the nature of reception. Preaching is not just about speaker performance but also profoundly about hearer reception. Do we have enough faith in the cross to trust the efficacy of the cross even though it goes verbally unspoken? Can we trust the efficacy of what we believe and say God truly works in the cross if we deliver that word in the same kind of suffering and compassionate silence that Jesus first carried it?

The first word of the cross was a virtually silent act of self-giving to violent and rebellious people who were unrepentant. Among the few words spoken from the cross were, "Forgive them, for they know not what they do." How often has the Spirit groaned these words because of our need to verbalize the word of the cross even when the situation of our hearers would have been better served by a different form of proclamation? How often would our preaching of the cross have been more so if done in silence?

Conclusion

What does it mean today that preaching's message is the cross? What does it mean to God, to preachers, to people who come from various social locations? Some have claimed that what we learn from Paul is that the cross is preaching's message and it is to be performed as a herald's duty, without regard to sophistic audience analysis, since that might dilute the "pure" proclamation. Paul cannot be pinned down so easily. His word of the cross was the word the prideful, divisive, and enthusiastic Corinthians needed to hear most in their particular situation, not in spite of it. Moreover, Paul's rhetorical artistry in dismissing his own performance reveals a profound irony that penetrates his ministry and reverberates through even the paradox of the gospel's message.

My discussion here of the preaching of the cross has been scandalously autobiographical. This is because of my growing conviction that none of our God-talk, gospel-talk, or cross-talk has much meaning apart from the concrete intersection that such "talk" has had in our real lives. I am aware of the dangerous implications and frequent abuses by preachers who allow their own stories and agendas to eclipse The Story and the gospel's agendas. But this is a risk that we must continue to take since we are called to be witnesses of and to a God about whom we do not merely have objective information, but with whom we have genuine struggle and at times intensely joyful experiences. This fragile and personal witness is finally what it means to preach the cross in light of the empty tomb. Such a word transcends mere code words, which warm an insulated community's prejudices. Such a word bears witness by and to the power of God's grace to a love that compassionately holds even the greatest of human affliction. Whether that word is one of protest, reconciliation, and forgiveness, or of silent presence, we offer it up as a sacrifice itself, in trust that it shall not return void, but will indeed accomplish that for which God in mercy continues to send and empower it.

8

Lament: Faith's Response to Loss

LAMENT HAS BEEN AN underutilized language of faith in Christian theology, worship, and preaching. In recent decades significant attempts have been made to revitalize faith by reclaiming the biblically and theologically rich resources of outcry, questioning, and articulated mournfulness.[1] This is somewhat ironic since lament has often been associated with the opposite of faith, namely doubt or even unbelief. There is a deep tradition in popular piety and theology that one ought not question God, and questioning is at the heart of the practice of lament.

This suspicion of lament is likely due to a kind of hyper-Calvinist leaning that believes that God is in control of everything that happens, indeed, even orchestrates every event, every minute, every last-second parking place. Such a belief in a micro-managing God behind history's mysterious curtain leads to a conclusion that any language of dissent would be a lack of faith, a challenge of God's providence, even a blasphemous clash with God's wisdom. Faith, instead, ought to acquiesce to God's will, which inexorably corresponds to reality as it is working its way out in the world and in our lives. If we experience pain, loss, violence, grief, or whatever, we must accept it as somehow God's will.

One Christian hymnodist, William Cowper, expressed this sentiment well in his hymn "God Moves in a Mysterious Way":

> God moves in a mysterious way,
> His wonders to perform;
> He plants His footsteps in the sea,
> And rides upon the storm.

---

1. See especially Powery, *Spirit Speech* and *Dem Dry Bones*; Brown and Miller, *Lament*; and Brueggemann, *Message of the Psalms*.

Lament: Faith's Response to Loss

Deep in unfathomable mines,
Of never-failing skill,
He treasures up His bright designs,
And works His sovereign will.

Ye fearful saints, fresh courage take,
The clouds ye so much dread,
Are big with mercy, and shall break,
In blessings on your head.

Judge not the Lord by feeble sense,
But trust Him for His grace;
Behind a frowning providence,
He hides a smiling face.

His purposes will ripen fast,
Unfolding every hour;
The bud may have a bitter taste,
But sweet will be the flower.

Blind unbelief is sure to err,
And scan his work in vain;
God is His own interpreter,
And He will make it plain.[2]

I grew up singing this hymn in worship, thinking that it artistically and triumphantly resolved the theodicy problem. Now many years later, having suffered loss of my own that I could not reconcile with a simple faith, and after reading more about what the author, Cowper, himself dealt with in his life, I now conclude that his hymn was a valiant effort on his part to reconcile his own life of loss, sorrow, and grief with his Calvinistic faith. His history of mental anguish, institutionalization, suicide attempts, and attempts through poetry and hymnody to reconcile the discrepancies of his existence and faith all could be interpreted to stem from a need to maintain faith in a God who is inexorably in control of every life event, even the death of five siblings in their infancy and the death of his beloved mother when he was only six years old.

When Cowper was fifty-eight years old his cousin, Ann Bodham, sent him a picture of his mother, which prompted his writing of the poem "On the Receipt of My Mother's Picture." A close reading shows a boy still torn

---

2. Cited from Howard, ed., *Songs of Faith and Praise*, hymn 26.

in two between the senseless loss of his mother when he was so young and a theology brokered to him that promised a neat and tidy resolution to loss and grief. Apparently, according to the poem, certain well-meaning attendants to the surviving Cowper children attempted to assuage William's bereavement:

> Thy maidens griev'd themselves at my concern,
> Oft gave me promise of a quick return.
> What ardently I wish'd, I long believ'd,
> And, disappointed still, was still deceiv'd;
> By disappointment every day beguil'd,
> Dupe of to-morrow even from a child.
> Thus many a sad to-morrow came and went,
> Till, all my stock of infant sorrow spent,
> I learn'd at last submission to my lot;
> But, though I less deplor'd thee, ne'er forgot.[3]

Cowper was tortured by his loss, which poignantly reveals itself through this lengthy poem fifty-two years after her death. The rigid confidence of the faith foisted upon him was something he struggled with "off camera," as shown in this honest outpouring, even if his hymns always ride a wave of unwavering confidence in God's providential wisdom and power.

The poem reveals that he ardently wished for the theological promises offered to him to be true, and he long believed them, yet that construct ultimately left him "disappointed," "deceived," and "beguiled," and in the end "duped" him. After many days and years of unfulfilled longing, the only option he seems to have seen in face of such a severe theology was to submit to it. He asserts that such submission led to less grief (perhaps), but he resolutely states that he nevertheless never forgot her.

Cowper's poetry and hymnody are powerful and prodigious. They often show raw emotion and struggle, but most often they color within the lines of orthodox Calvinistic theological propriety. No other theological option seemed to be available to him. Of course the Bible, with its rich theological variety, seems to have been tantalizingly close by, but this is another tale of the hermeneutical predispositions that allow certain parts of Scripture to light up while other parts remain dark. The biblical cries of lament didn't fit Cowper's theological criteria. Paul's apocalyptic gospel, with its insistence on the now-but-not-yet character of faith and God's work in the gospel, did not register on his theological radar. One can only wonder

---

3. Quoted from http://www.poetryfoundation.org/poem/173287.

Lament: Faith's Response to Loss

what impact Cowper could have had on the history of hymnody, and thus on Christian worship and spirituality, if his interpretive lens of discretion had been different, if his real-life struggle of faith in the face of loss could have found voice in the biblically shaped faith of lament and the apocalyptic gospel.

Cowper's voice, however, has been the dominant one in the language of the church's hymns. Certain theological presuppositions in the hymnic tradition have been immovable, and those positions have in turn formed objections to the legitimacy of lament as a viable language of faith and thus of hymnody, arguably one of the most important ways the church articulates its theology and faith. Let's examine some of these objections.

> *Objection 1: Haven't the New Testament and the resurrection of Jesus effectively eliminated the need for lament? Aren't the anguished cries that we see in the Old Testament superseded—indeed, rendered unnecessary—in light of the gospel? Might those cries even be seen as a sign of unbelief in the gospel now that God has raised Jesus from the dead?*

These questions assume a kind of triumphalist gospel, or realized eschatology. They attempt to eliminate the tension in Christian existence, in life lived between the times of Jesus' first coming and his promised second coming. In Jesus' resurrection the New Age has dawned, but the Day has yet to fully arrive. Death has been conquered by Jesus' death and resurrection. Those in Christ have been raised to new life in him, yet the general resurrection yet waits his return. The apocalyptic character of the gospel means that the full benefits of God's Reign are only partial now; they are now-but-not-yet. The church is thus the eschatological community that bears witness to its proleptically resurrected state in its counter–old age existence, by breaking barriers of racism, sexism, and ageism, and making justice, keeping justice, and resisting the powers that bring violence and death to God's creatures and God's creation. Part of the church's linguistic task, therefore, is to protest against the powers as well as offer persistent prayer that God bring about the promised but as-yet-unfulfilled completion of what God has begun in Jesus' death and resurrection. Until that moment of consummation, the cry of "*Maranatha!*"—"Come Lord Jesus!"—is as much a prayer of hope as of anguish for a cessation to the embarrassment of history and the suffering that continues in the time of waiting for God's long-promised rectification.

> *Objection 2: Isn't the act of lament an act of raising questions for which believers have the answer? In Christ isn't there an answer for every question?*

On one level it may be true to call what God has done in Jesus' death and resurrection an answer to the question, or problem, of a broken-down creation in desperate need of rectification, renewal and re-creation. But that answer is one that is not visible to the naked eye. Jesus' own resurrection remains hidden to the canons of historical inquiry, relegated instead to witnesses now long dead. As it is, the church continues to exist on the fumes of that initial witness—an amazing fact so far down the road of time. Lament, as the outcry of the bereaved and, especially in Christ, as the outrage of those who ache for the fulfillment of the promise, is the very kind of persistent, verbalized faith that we see Jesus praising in the parable of the widow and the unjust judge (18:1–8). Because Jesus has not returned, the final curtain on history and eternity has not been drawn back to reveal to all that God has done. Thus, God's work is visible only through a mirror dimly, embraced by faith or rejected by unbelief.

The embrace of this unseen vision does not, however, mean an acquiescence of faith's desire for the completion of what God has begun. In fact, I would argue that true belief in the vision projected in the apocalyptic gospel creates prophetic outrage at the gap that exists between the promise and the fulfillment.

One form this prophetic outrage takes is lament: the anguished and honest cry of grief, the agonized and questioning spirit that asks God "Why?" and "How long?" Because it is only on the day of Christ's return that we will "see face to face," and thus understand what we cannot know now, the so-called "Christian answer" of Jesus' resurrection, when sprinkled like a magic potion on any and all instances of suffering and loss, ends up more often than not increasing the weight of grief rather than being a source of comfort. Even the "answer" must await its proper time and context. Jesus' own resurrection could only occur after his death. Each of the Gospel writers leads us on the long and dusty road to Jerusalem, painstakingly taking us through the events of the betrayal, the trial, the crucifixion, the death, and the burial of Jesus before telling us the miracle of the resurrection early

Lament: Faith's Response to Loss

Sunday morning. None begin with "He is risen!" We can be pretty certain that the Apostle Paul would not have shouted his triumphal words "Where, O death, is your victory? Where, O death, is your sting?" in a children's cancer ward. Pastoral sensitivity to the in-between-time predicament of all creatures and all creation recognizes that the good news declaration of resurrection is sometimes best whispered through clenched teeth in the very real, poignant face of this world's travail.

On another level, when the "answer" of resurrection is taken to be a quick fix to any and every situation of loss and grief, it underestimates the role and function of the question in the person who is struggling with loss. To paraphrase Holocaust survivor Elie Wiesel, "There is a certain power in the question which isn't to be found in any answer."[4] It is the power of the question that lament explores. If that questioning is squelched in the life of the sufferer or the community of faith, an essential and necessary process, both psychologically and theologically, is thwarted and stunted.

Objection 3: But if Jesus' followers really believed in the resurrection, if they really believed in the power of God to overcome evil and provide joy and comfort in his Spirit, then lament wouldn't be needed. Maybe laments are for those who just cannot believe as they ought.

This is to sidetrack the real issue. The issue is not whether or not one believes in the resurrection, or how strongly one believes in it. The issue is how one who believes deeply in the resurrection copes now, every day, with the painful absence of an important relationship, while waiting for the time in which all wrongs will eventually be righted.

The lament is the response of one who cares enough to take the tragic and the meaningless before God. That is an act of faith. To take our honest questions to God is not an act of defamation toward the character of God, but an act of affirmation. Why are there wrongs in this in-between time? Why are they so severe? How long must we endure? These are cries within the context of the faith struggle in this in-between time. And if Christians can muster at least as much faith as the Old Testament psalmist and prophets, then the release of such questions finds its form in lament.

---

4. Wiesel, *Night*, 16.

This idea is well expressed by Nicholas Wolterstorff in his *Lament for a Son*:

> Elements of the gospel that I always thought would console (me) did not. They did something else, but not that. It did not console me to be reminded of the hope of resurrection. If I had forgotten that hope, then it would indeed have brought light into my life to be reminded of it. But I did not think of death as a bottomless pit. I did not grieve as one who has no hope. Yet Eric is gone, here and now he is gone; now I cannot talk with him, now I cannot see him, now I cannot hug him, now I cannot hear of his plans for the future. That is my sorrow. A friend said, "Remember, he's in good hands." I was deeply moved. But that reality does not put Eric back in my hands now. That's my grief. For that grief, what consolation can there be other than having him back? . . . when death is seen as the slicing off of what God declared to be, and what all of us feel to be, of great worth, then death is—well, not friend, but enemy. Though I shall indeed recall that death is being overcome, my grief is that death still stalks this world and one day knifed down my Eric.
>
> Nothing fills the void of his absence. He is not replaceable. We can't just go out and get another just like him.[5]

Death is not gone. Sin is still among us. Creation is not at rest since resurrection Sunday. If anything, resurrection Sunday seems to have made the ripples of unrest in the creation grow more violent. Creation groans as a woman in the throes of hard labor, longing for its own delivery. And if we are honest, we must admit that "in our spirits we, too, groan as we await full adoption. And the Spirit intercedes with sighs too deep for words," Paul says, as our hearts are poured out like wax in our in-between-time struggle. We still pray legitimately "Thy Kingdom come!" because it isn't all here yet. And because death and sin are still realities in this in-between-time as we await the fulfillment of God's Kingdom, there is loss, and loss stings. And if we, out of some limited biblical theology of glory, tell people in or out of the church that their feelings of loss and grief are unnecessary because of the resurrection, or the Spirit, or heaven's superior blessedness to earth, then we have robbed them, and ourselves, of the presence and power of God now in our lives.

Robert Davidson, a Scottish Presbyterian who taught at the University of Glasgow, has written an important book entitled *The Courage to Doubt*. In the first chapter he analyzes Israel's hymnbook, the book of Psalms, and

---

5. Wolterstorff, *Lament for a Son*, 31–32.

Lament: Faith's Response to Loss

The Church Hymnary (3rd ed., 1973), which the Church of Scotland and other Presbyterian churches use. He observes that of the various types of Old Testament psalms the greatest percent is of individual or personal laments. If these are combined with the psalms of community lament, they make up almost half of Israel's ancient hymnbook. Davidson tries to explain the significance of this for Israel's religious faith:

> Such psalms found a lasting place in the hymnbook of ancient Israel and were continuingly used and useful because both the community and individuals within the community found across the centuries that serious threats to the integrity of their religious experience had to be faced. In every age faith involved a struggle, a struggle to understand the ways of the God whose presence was celebrated in worship, but who often seemed strangely absent. "Why" and "How long" were repeatedly discovered to be as authentic cries as "Hallelujah!"[6]

Davidson notes that in *The Church Hymnary* 58 of the 150 biblical psalms are used as hymns. Sixty-four percent of those retained are psalms of adoration, praise, thanksgiving, or confidence. Only four community laments are included, but two of these by selective editing have been turned into hymns of praise. Only ten personal psalms of lament are included, and these have undergone selective editing as well. Psalms of bitter anguish and the raw struggle of faith before God have been transformed into pious hymns of confession. Only two personal laments have retained their original meaning: Psalm 22, most of which we are very familiar with because Jesus echoed this lament, and Psalm 42. "The net result," Davidson concludes, "is that out of forty-one psalms of personal lament only two remain intact, both of them because of christological associations."[7]

When we look in the *The Church Hymnary*'s index, we find the following categories of hymns: Adoration and Thanksgiving, Affirmation, Dedication and Discipleship, Stewardship and Service, Witness and Encouragement, Intercession, and The Church Triumphant. Most of these themes find their parallel in the Old Testament psalms, but we find nothing to mirror the psalms' wealth of lament prayers and hymns. "For that we would have to include a section entitled 'Questioning and Protest.'"[8]

---

6. Davidson, *Courage to Doubt*, 12.
7. Ibid., 14.
8. Ibid., 15.

PART 2—PROCLAIMING GOD'S REIGN IN A WORLD THAT IS PASSING AWAY

Davidson observes, "There is no hymnbook known to me in current use which questions faith so seriously and consistently as the Psalms; no hymnbook which so openly encourages people to live through, in the context of worship, the dark night of their soul."[9]

With the use of H. Gunkel's categorizations of the Psalms,[10] I examined one denominational hymnal as a test case, *Great Songs of the Church*, edited by Forrest McCann. My study showed that it uses ninety-nine of the Old Testament psalms, whereas the Scottish hymnal used fifty-eight. Of those ninety-nine, no community laments are appropriated from the Psalms. Eleven individual laments are appropriated. All eleven have been selectively edited, usually down to one verse. None of the eleven in their edited fashion voice any lament. So of the one-hundred and fifty psalms, almost half of which are lament-laden in their canonical context, ninety-nine psalms are used in this hymnbook, yet none voice any shred of lament. In fact, the general tenor of the hymns indicate that lament is not appropriate behavior for a Christian.

Here are two examples of that theological repositioning of those psalms, though many more could be cited. The first, "O, for a Faith That Will Not Shrink" (#505), has worshippers sing that they have a faith "that will not murmur or complain, beneath the chastening rod; but in the hour of grief or pain will lean upon its God." Leaning upon God is a good, faithful thing to do. But, according to the other stanzas, the leaning must not take the form of questioning or lament. Perhaps a better wording for the hymn, if we were to use the psalmist's own theology as our voice and example, would be, "O, for a faith that will not shrink, but loud complains and lifts its voice beneath the chastening rod; and in the hour of grief or pain *thus* leans upon its God."

The other (#555) reads, "Here we are but straying pilgrims; Here our path is often dim; But to cheer us on our journey, Still we sing this wayside hymn: Yonder over the rolling river, where the shining mansions rise, Soon will be our home forever, And the smile of the blessed Giver Gladdens all our longing eyes." The refrain of this song illustrates our alternative to lament. Heaven and heaven's hope have replaced the cry of the sufferer in the present. The now is cashed in for an exclusive look at the then. We need to raise the question as to what this does to our faith, what this says about covenant and about our relationship with God. A heavy heart needs, from

---

9. Ibid.
10. Gunkel, *Einleitung in die Psalmen*.

Lament: Faith's Response to Loss

both a psychological and theological vantage point, to express itself in ways other than the ways that most of our hymns are written.

The writer of Proverbs knew that "He who sings songs to a heavy heart is like one who takes off a garment on a cold day, and like vinegar on a wound" (25:20). The psalmist, speaking at perhaps the most incongruous time in Israel's history (the Babylonian exile), writes in Psalm 137, "By the waters of Babylon, there we sat down and wept, when we remembered Zion. On the willows we hung up our lyres. For there our captors required of us songs, and our tormentors, mirth, saying, 'Sing us one of the songs of Zion!' How shall we sing the Lord's song in a foreign land?" There are reasons for this loss of lament and its replacement with "happy" songs of heaven. And they are theological reasons. But we need to recognize them as emendations of the biblically oriented language of lament due to a felt need to tone down the raw vigor of the biblical traditions, developments of supposed piousness and orthodoxy that, in fact, have little to do with a biblically grounded faith.

J. M. Powis Smith has noted that hymnbooks undergo change to keep step with the "aesthetic and theological standards of our own day."[11] But Davidson is quick to note the "real danger that 'the aesthetic and theological standards of our day'—which may indeed lead us to recoil from the raw vigour of some of the psalms—may at the same time mislead us into neglecting continuingly important aspects of the faith we inherit."[12] Davidson alludes to the possibility that a truncated canon, a shrunken worship liturgy, and a lopsided proclamation of the word in preaching have in essence created a much greater need for psychotherapy, personal awareness and growth, and self-help groups. He quotes a psychotherapist who issues this warning to the church: "For the most part the churches have not yet learned that the best way to pass from defensive rationalizations to secure faith is to let doubts, inconsistencies, confusions and rebellions come out into the open instead of using various forms of spiritual coercion to keep them hidden or to draw them from awareness altogether."[13]

There is indeed something to be learned just here from the field of psychology. If it has taught us anything, it is that the root problem behind most neuroses and psychoses is repression. Freud, of course, said that the basic human repression out of which spring all the problems of humankind

---

11. As quoted by Davidson, *Courage to Doubt*, 16.
12. Ibid.
13. Ibid., 17.

is sexual repression. But more recently Ernest Becker, in his Pulitzer Prize–winning book *The Denial of Death*, has argued that it is not the repression of sex that is humanity's basic problem, but the repression of death. By "death" Becker means the broad spectrum of death in human existence: from anxiety about our own personal deaths, to the loss of family and friends, to the experience of loss that takes place almost constantly every day all around us. We are in a constant state of losing, and we have been since childhood. Our American culture doesn't help our already inclined tendencies to deny experiences of loss in life. It encourages the lie that becomes our reality because we can't face true existence. Becker writes, "Modern man is drinking and drugging himself out of awareness, or he spends his time shopping, which is the same thing."[14]

The world is not unaware of the fact that it is decaying and dying. With the new technology in health and skin care, we can all live ten years longer and look twenty years younger when we die. An increasingly common way that our society is dealing with the problem of human aging is cosmetic surgery. Los Angeles seems to be on the cutting edge of this phenomenon, but it has worked its way all across the country.

Erma Bombeck[15] tells of a lunch she was having in Philadelphia when she observed four little old ladies at a table next to her. The first thing she noticed was the surprised expression on each of their faces. She mused to herself that if the stock market were to crash again not one of them would even be able to blink. And as she looked more closely, she figured that there had been enough nips, tucks, and pinches among the four of them to make up a fifth person. The world is very aware that it is dying. Its problem is that it continues to look for ways to avoid, to deny, that reality.

A faith that is nurtured in the breadth, length, height, and depth of the rich tradition of Scripture is a faith that is able to face life's vicissitudes. A faith that is willing to embrace the fullness of its theological heritage is a faith that is willing, in turn, to be embraced by the tradition in such a way that one's existence now is made meaningful and livable even in the times of distress. This means the willingness to embrace the biblical traditions of lament and the rich responses to exile. To embrace these traditions is to embrace again our God as a God who listens.[16] How many times have we read in Scripture, "I have heard your cries" or "Your cries have come to

---

14. Becker, *Denial of Death*, 284.
15. See Bombeck, "When Does One Reach Age of Freedom to Eat?"
16. See Birch, "Biblical Faith," 966.

Lament: Faith's Response to Loss

me"? Dorothée Soelle in her book *Suffering* suggests that the outcry of the sufferer is the beginning of healing. If the church does not permit those who are suffering to voice outcry, it would be complicit in thwarting the healing process of sufferers. Could it be that in the wisdom of God Israel's early hymnbook (the Psalms) was as psychologically relevant as it was theologically balanced for a people struggling on the bumpy road of life?

The Psalms invite us to weep. They invite us to wail, to cry out in the face of wrong, injustice, and meaningless loss, "Why, O God?" and "How long?" They help us find the words when no words will do. Indeed, the Psalms function in the community of faith as prayer's speech teacher. They train our voices and lead us into the full range of spiritual and emotional expression before God. Some of these laments are unconventional, even "unorthodox," according to our "aesthetic and theological standards." Some have even been called "un-evangelical prayers." They are such because they are raw, honest, and seemingly unedited. But what if they are highly stylized expressions of the reality of faith in the face of loss? They threaten the evangelical prayer police but only because they are not comfortable with unanswered questions, open-ended suffering, and honest questioning of God. It does not appear from the biblical literature itself, however, that God is threatened or upset by such honest wrestling in prayer.

Of the psalms of lament, Bruce Birch writes:

> Anger, bitterness, despair, doubt—it is all there, not because the tradition desires to affirm those expressions as ends in themselves, but because if the pain is not exposed, the healing cannot begin. These Psalms are shocking to us because so much of our own worship tries to conceal our deepest wounds. Our own worship so often takes place at the level of the lowest common denominator of our corporate experience.[17]

"If the pain is not exposed, the healing cannot begin." It is precisely here that I believe the Old Testament may make its most valuable contribution to the contemporary community of faith. For it is here that we are allowed to face and voice our deepest fears, angers, doubts, and desires. It is a painful journey, yet a journey of pain that opens up the true and viable vistas of joy in pain's midst. It is on this path that we learn the true nature of biblical joy. That is the joy that Paul speaks of in Philippians when he says, " Rejoice in the Lord always. I will say it again: Rejoice!" (Phil 4:4, NIV). Do we remember that as Paul wrote these words in the "joyful"

17. Ibid.

letter to Philippi, most likely he sat in a dark, damp prison cell in Rome, with only one appointment on his calendar—a meeting with the tyrannical Emperor Nero? The joy of which Paul speaks is a joy of wholeness and spiritual health that outward circumstances do not control, cannot touch. It is no coincidence that this joy of wholeness and spiritual health is one of the ways to define the word "salvation." Salvation is not a turning away from anything in life for some dim future bliss; rather, salvation is a facing of life—all of it—and coming through it by the mighty and outstretched hand of God.

The biblical laments help expose our pain, give that pain voice, and thus lay the foundation for healing to begin. In December 1986 I found myself in an emergency room with my son lying on a cold table, finally and hurriedly hooked up to machines that made only one sound, a high-pitched continuous beep. It was the most horrifying sound I ever heard in my life. It reduced me to a heap of nothingness on the floor. Everything in my world had tumbled. All words and thoughts failed me. I felt utterly lost. It was in this context that words from the Old Testament began my articulation. I had no words. The words that started to form on my lips (and I could think of no others) were David's words. His grief spoke where my grief did not know where to begin.

David knew what it was to lose sons. Sometimes we treat David's loss of sons lightly because Absalom was a scoundrel and Bathsheba's baby was a result of scandal. But to David, they were his boys. In 2 Samuel 18 David cared less about the battle than about his son, even though the son was trying to usurp his throne.

> The king said to the Cushite, "Is it well with the young man Absalom?" The Cushite answered, "May the enemies of my lord the king, and all who rise up to do you harm, be like that young man."
>
> The king was deeply moved, and went up to the chamber over the gate, and wept; and as he went, he said, "O my son Absalom, my son, my son Absalom! Would I had died instead of you, O Absalom, my son, my son!"

There I was, cradled on the one side by these words of lament in Scripture, as they tried to give me some support in the face of my loss, as they tried to give my pain some form of verbal articulation. And on the other side I was cradled by the contemporary community of faith in the person of my elder, teacher, friend, and co-participant in grief, Jim Roberts. He held me through his own tears, tears forged from his own experience of loss ten

Lament: Faith's Response to Loss

years earlier in the person of his son, Nathaniel. He urged me to speak. He urged me to cry and to moan. He assured me it was okay to say all that my broken heart could utter. And as I looked up at him, all I could say was, "I feel... I feel... I feel what you felt." And we both wept.

Held by the community of faith, past and present, the future was still a murky mirror holding out the hope for reunion and reconciliation. I did not doubt that. But in the awfulness of the moment of loss, future joy seemed to mock more than comfort. There shall be no more death or tears then, according to John on Patmos (Rev 21:4), but now, while we wait for that day, we weep. I was still a heap and worthless in my moment of loss, but the community held me, comforted me, and started forming on my lips the beginnings of articulation that would lead to healing. I had a context in which to heal: the community of faith, both in Scripture and in the person of Jim—and neither would let me go. I was not falling into nothing. I was falling, due to my loss and grief, into the context of the covenant community, a community formed and held together by its, as yet, unfinished gospel.

Ultimately and ironically, comfort and consolation come from looking into the face of our painful losses and not away from them. Diogenes Allen, in his *Traces of God in a Frequently Hostile World*, writes, "It is not by turning our backs on the harsh realities of life that we can find help in our daily lives, but by facing them, so that we do not merely keep our dreams of personal happiness alive, but learn what happiness really is."[18] Henri Nouwen, in a letter to his father six months after Henri's mother died, wrote:

> Is this consolation? Does this bring comfort? It appears that I am doing the opposite of bringing comfort. Maybe so. Maybe these words will only increase your tears and deepen your grief. But for me, your son, who grieves with you, there is no other way. I want to comfort and console you, but not in a way that covers up real pain and avoids all wounds. I am writing you this letter in the firm conviction that reality can be faced and entered with an open mind and an open heart, and in the sincere belief that consolation and comfort are to be found where our wounds hurt most.[19]

Nicholas Wolterstorff's book *Lament for a Son*, following his son Eric's tragic death, is really a peek into his diary, a look at the reflections of a sincere Christian who was face to face with the greatest tragedy that he

---

18. Allen, *Traces of God*, 2.
19. Nouwen, *Letter of Consolation*, 17.

had ever known. In his state of grief Wolterstorff resolved that to look away from such an experience of profound loss would be unfaithfulness.

> I skimmed some books on grief. They offered ways of not looking at death and pain in the face, ways of turning away from death out there to one's own inner "grief process," and then on that laying on the heavy hand of rationality. I will not have it so. I will not look away. I will indeed remind myself that there is more to life than pain. I will accept joy. But I will not look away from Eric dead. Its demonic awfulness I will not ignore. I owe that—to him and God.[20]

I find it revealing that Wolterstorff, a Christian philosopher at Yale, says at one point in his reflections, "Faith endures, but my address to God is uncomfortably, perplexingly, altered."[21] Wolterstorff struggles in his attempt to come before God when the pain of his loss is so central to his conscious being. To come before God when overwhelming grief seems irremovably in the way demands a different kind of approach. Wolterstorff says:

> I must explore The Lament as a mode for my address to God. Psalm 42 is a lament in the context of a faith that endures. Lament and trust are in tension, like wood and string in (a) bow. "My tears have been my food day and night," says the song writer. I remember, he says, how it was when joy was still my lot, "how I used to go with the multitude, leading the procession to the house of God with shouts of joy and thanksgiving among the festive throng." Now it's different. I am downcast, disturbed. Yet I find that faith is not dead. So I say to myself, "Put your hope in God, for I will yet praise him, my Savior and my God." But then my grief returns and again I lament to God my Rock: "Why have you forgotten me? Why must I go about mourning, oppressed by the enemy?" Again faith replies: "Put your hope in God, for I will yet praise him, my Savior and my God." Back and forth, lament and faith, faith and lament, each fastened to the other. A bruised faith, a longing faith, a faith emptied of nearness: "As a deer pants for streams of water, so my soul pants for you, O God. My soul thirsts for God, for the living God. When can I go and meet with God?" Yet in the distance of endurance I join the song: "By day the Lord directs his love, at night his song is with me—a prayer to the God of my life."[22]

---

20. Wolterstorff, *Lament for a Son*, 54.
21. Ibid., 70.
22. Ibid., 70–71.

Lament: Faith's Response to Loss

Thus we hear the song of lament in a contemporary Christian's tones toward God, tones that struggle to maintain the relationship with God even now when loss has shaken faith's foundations to the core. And it is in a psalm of lament that a window for faith to endure opens. That is grace!

The problems of pain, suffering, loss, and death present us with questions in regard to God's presence—or maybe more accurately, in regard to God's absence. By ignoring the texts of lament and dissent, we limit our perspective of faith. If the Spirit was an integral prompter of not only Scripture's words in their initial inception, as well as a companion to David and his fellow compatriots of faith, might our erasure of their grappling words of faith in the face of loss not be another way we quench the Spirit today?

I sometimes wonder if preachers are themselves capable of lament and are capable of leading our people in faithful lament. The problem is that if we as pastoral leaders are incapable, or are perceived as being incapable, of lamenting in the face of loss, we lose a crucial place of significance and relevance to the world and to the suffering people within our churches—people who know very well that death, pain, grief, and loss are real and must be faced. If the people of God are to be freed to the potentially healing processes of grief through honest lament, it is the responsibility of ministerial leaders to lead the people in the grieving process, and in faithful practices of lament, even and especially in worship, a place where lament has traditionally been forbidden.

Elie Wiesel, in his book *The Madness of God*, pictures a pastoral leader who has the opportunity and potential to lead his people in liturgical protest against the powers of death and loss:

> The year was 1965. On Yom Kippur eve I found myself somewhere in Russia, in a synagogue crowded with people. . . . All around me were elderly, defeated-looking men. . . . My own eyes were glued to the handsome but seemingly lifeless face of the Rabbi. An ancestral, bewildering sadness emanated from his person. He seemed to be living elsewhere, resigned, beyond hope, foundering into a faraway past, even, perhaps, into oblivion. Suddenly a mad thought crossed my mind: Something is about to happen; any moment now the Rabbi will wake up, shake himself, pound the pulpit and cry out, shout his pain, his rage, his truth. I felt the tension building up inside me; the wait was becoming unbearable. But nothing happened. The old man remained prisoner of his past, out of his fear. Tall but stooped, the old Rabbi was reciting the customary litanies, oblivious of his surroundings. From time to time

his unseeing gaze wandered over the faithful. And all the while I was addressing him soundlessly, pleading with him, my heart beating wildly as though in expectation of a storm long abrewing, a drama about to unfold. I begged the old man: Do something, free yourself tonight and you will enter our people's legend; let the hushed reality buried inside you for so many years explode; speak out, say what oppresses you—one cry, just one, will be enough to bring down the walls that encircle and crush you. My eyes pleaded with him, prodded him. In vain. For him it was too late. He had suffered too much, endured too many ordeals for too many years. He no longer had the strength to imagine himself free.[23]

Pain can close up the bowels of lament so that we wither up and die. The community of faith, rooted and grounded in the fullness of its speech (that is, its theological and scriptural traditions) to God, has the resources in that tradition to enter pain, loss, and death, and through faithful lament to live through it, learning to embrace life again.

In an episode of *The Women of Brewster Place* a couple was arguing in a room adjacent to their young daughter. The girl saw a bug come through the cracks in the wall around a light socket, so she went over to explore the bug and its home. She grabbed a metal object and began probing around the socket. It was only a matter of seconds before her parents heard the electric shock and the last cry of their daughter.

The next scene is at the home of the couple after the funeral. Throngs of people gathered and food piled up all over the place. Everyone was in black. The mother sat motionless in bed. One of her friends urged her to eat. Someone muttered, "She's young; she can have others." "I lost a child twenty years ago; she'll get over it." Another friend continued to go up to the bereaving mother saying, "Come on now, honey, you've got to keep your strength up. Now eat something." The mother stared straight out into nowhere, pale and weak. One of the women at the house, played by Oprah Winfrey, saw this scene and kept her eye on the mother. The friend urging food on the grieving mother eventually gave up and went to the potluck line next to Oprah, commenting, "She just won't do a thing I say. She really ought to eat something."

Two days passed. The Oprah character came over to the grieving woman's house. She opened the door without knocking and stood in the doorway. The woman inside was growing more and more pale, apparently

---

23. Wiesel, *Zalman*, 1–2.

Lament: Faith's Response to Loss

having lost her will to live. Oprah declared, "If you're gonna leave this world, you're gonna have to do it over my dead body!"

Oprah went into the bedroom, physically got into bed with the woman, and put her arms completely around her. She started rocking her firmly but with an unmistakably loving concern. As she rocked, she began saying firmly, and very persistently, "Come back! Come Back!" After some time her volume had come down, but her rhythmic rocking and the depth of her pleading were haunting. You knew she wasn't going anywhere and you knew she wasn't going to give up on her. It looked like a mother rocking an oversized infant. And after a long while the mother of the dead girl began to weep, slowly, and softly at first. Eventually, her weeping turned into wailing and she then began to articulate her outrage: "Why did I have to lose my little girl?" Why, O God? Why?" In that moment her healing began. Her life had begun again.

The role of the lament in the life of the community of faith is the role that Oprah fulfilled in this story. When we are enveloped in the biblical lament, and especially when we are in the context of the covenant community of faith, we have, as it were, a bracket of perspective surrounding us in and through which God works. We are not left alone but we are swept up, rocked, and called back to live now. We are given a context and words for our weeping. And in that context of asking the great questions of our lives and wailing with what seems like our life's last breath, we come to realize that the one who rocks us and beckons us back from giving up is the present God, who himself laments with us.

Conclusion

WHAT FILLS THE SPACE between Jesus' first and second comings into this world? If we are honest about what we see all around us, it is quite a mixed bag. Our world is a vast realm of wonder and terror.

On one side of the globe a family vacationing on pure white beaches schedules an afternoon of snorkeling amid startlingly beautiful reefs. On the other side of the world, women and girls are divided from the men and boys in their families at gunpoint. The men are summarily murdered. The women are catalogued and sold into the sex slavery market, where insidiously a "theology of rape" justifies the violence done to them in the name of God and spirituality.[1]

What is the church's response to a such mixed bag of realities? There have been many differing answers to that question. The response that I have made here is multipronged. First, the church is the community in the world that has embraced the message of Jesus in the New Testament—the gospel—as God's response to what has gone wrong with the world. It sees in God's invasion, in Jesus' person, of a co-opted creation a radical taking back of what came from God and belongs to God. The gospel sounds forth God's hostile takeover of a creation that has been stolen by forces seen and unseen that have rebelled against God's will and way. Jesus' presence in the world, as depicted in the Gospels, shows us what God wills for God's creation: healing, wholeness, community, and a dismantling of oppressive structures and oppressing ways of human being and relating. Jesus' presence signals the beginning of Satan's end. Jesus' death begins the end of the old age. And just as Jesus' death begins to shut the door on the age of death, violence, and terror, Jesus' resurrection begins to open the door to the New Age of

---

1. See Callimachi, "ISIS Enshrines a Theology of Rape."

God's shalom, peace, wholeness, healing, and life eternal. Simultaneously, the curtain on the first act closes as the curtain rises on the second.

Second, the church is the community that has a foot in both worlds, the old and the New. As such it has a peculiar witness and existence. Its witness consists of forming language that is appropriate to its conflicting experiences of suffering and hope, death and life, fear and faith. In order for that witness not to be a kind of spiritual coercion, a language of denial in face of a reality of ongoing misery in so much of this world's experience, the church champions the language of lament, protest, outcry, and questioning—of both this world's hateful ways and of God's prolonged absence. Made to praise God, but mired in a world of suffering and death that thwarts praise, the church recognizes creation's precarious disjuncture and joins with the Spirit in helping articulate this disjuncture through the language of lament. Lament becomes the Spirit's work in and through a creation and its creatures who ache for God's conclusion, for God's ultimate rectification. Praise erupts, too, here and there, not as a language of denial, but as an anticipatory and visionary grasping of the promise of God.

Third, the church begins to instantiate, in the here and now, the justice and shalom of God that she knows is creation's ultimate destiny due to the death and resurrection of Jesus. His resurrection is the first fruits of a resurrection that will ultimately mean life to all who have died, of a healing and wholeness that will come to a weary and broken creation and all her creatures. The mission of the church in this in-between time is to put in place the same structures and situations of justice, peace, inclusion, love, mercy, and wholeness that she knows that God will bring about in the consummation. The church thus lives its life by the motto, "*What will happen, can happen.*" As the eschatological community—that community of the end time—she lives an italicized existence, one that *leans toward a future* that she longs for, and one that she believes God is bringing to her from a realm yet unseen.

Thus the church lives out of the powerful resources that the gospel itself gives her. Yet that existence is precarious, since it is frustratingly perched between two worlds, one that is passing away and the other that is dawning. Faith looks toward the horizon of God's coming Kingdom. But it is also honest about the friction of the present and the frequently jarring effect of incompleteness. Honesty and hope create a tug of war within the heart and the mind. Thus, though a seeming contradiction, the church's

Conclusion

voice sometimes tells the truth in lament, outcry, and questioning, and sometimes in dramatic vision casting of a world on the horizon.

The final part of this book's title, *The Persistence of the Gospel*, is not just a theological claim that I assert. It is a confession of faith based on the gospel's persistent claim on my own life. That I have completed this book is testimony to God's unfailing persistence to not let me go, even though I despaired of life altogether when my firstborn son died on December 7, 1986. Now almost thirty years since that earthquake in my personal and spiritual life, I write these concluding words to a book about God's persistence through preaching and the Spirit on my son's thirtieth birthday, August 19, 2015. As every parent who has lost a child knows, the grief of this day, and all the intervening days that would have been shared—the birthdays, the Thanksgivings, the Christmases, the graduations, wedding, birth of grandchildren, the highs and lows, all of it—are grieved as never having been lived together. There is always a hole where he would have been, a silence where his voice would have spoken. And that void deepens the ache and longing for God to bring about what God has begun and promised to complete. And surprisingly, in my case, it has been the experience of hearing and seeing the preaching of the gospel through the apocalypse of African-American preachers that has uniquely kept my hope and faith kindled and burning for God's promised future. Let me explain a little further.

Since 2004 I have been teaching preaching at a historically, and still predominantly, African-American seminary in the southwestern part of the United States. We are not long removed from the Civil War, and even shorter removed from the civil rights era. The remnants and tensions of both lie all around. I've learned a lot about preaching in this environment over the last twelve years. One of the things that I've come to cherish in particular is the move in some black preaching where the preacher ascends into an ecstatic celebration.[2]

From the perspective of the apocalyptic gospel, I have come to see the sermonic climax point of celebration in black preaching to be that moment when actual *apocalypse*—revelation—happens. The climactic moment in the sermon, when the preacher reaches fever pitch, is when the preacher sees, if only for a brief moment, through the veil to the other side. Captured by the resplendent vision of God's coming Kingdom of shalom, healing,

---

2. Many, including especially Henry Mitchell (*Black Preaching*) and Frank Thomas (*They Like to Never Quit Praisin' God*), have done a masterful job in examining, explaining, and plotting this rhythmic movement.

Conclusion

freedom, and victory, dramatic ecstasy is the only appropriate action and verbalization. The congregation rides the wave of the preacher's vision, and verbal and bodily ecstasy, sometimes so captured by it that they glimpse the vision too, and fall out in laughter, tears, joy, and other verbal and nonverbal means of accompaniment and response. The frenzy is confusing to some, threatening to others, orchestrated perhaps by some who understand the rhetoric but not the reality.

But I have seen and heard some who, in that moment, see something of the truth and reality of God's promised future. Their voices and bodies become servants of the vision. They become conduits of the apocalyptic vision.

In what is probably his second most famous sermonic address, the Rev. Dr. Martin Luther King Jr. exhibited this revelatory moment in the sermon's climax. His words in that moment are, of course, words tied to a very specific social, political, and religious context in American civil rights history. Yet, it is remarkable how, in their character as proclamation of the apocalyptic gospel, they transcend that moment and become words and vision that many can relate to in their own situations of suffering and uncertainty. His words capture the gospel's persistent vision and hope in a world where fear and death threaten to smother faith.

> Well, I don't know what will happen now.
> We've got some difficult days ahead.
> But it really doesn't matter with me now, because I've been to the mountaintop.
> And I don't mind. Like anybody, I would like to live a long life.
> Longevity has its place.
> But I'm not concerned about that now.
> I just want to do God's will.
> And He's allowed me to go up to the mountain.
> And I've looked over.
> And I've seen the Promised Land.
> I may not get there with you.
> *But I want you to know tonight,*
> *that we, as a people, will get to the promised land!*
> *And so I'm happy, tonight.*
> *I'm not worried about anything.*
> *I'm not fearing any man!*
> *Mine eyes have seen the glory of the coming of the Lord!!*[3]

---

3. "I've Been to the Mountaintop," in King, *Testament of Hope*, 286.

Bibliography

Allen, Diogenes. *The Traces of God in a Frequently Hostile World*. Cambridge: Cowley, 1981.
Allen, Ronald. *Interpreting the Gospel: An Introduction to Preaching*. St. Louis: Chalice, 1998.
Augustine. *On Christian Doctrine*. New York: Pearson, 1958.
Barth, Karl. *Homiletics*. Translated by Donald E. Daniels and Geoffrey W. Bromiley. Louisville: Westminster John Knox, 1991.
Bauer, Walter, and F. Wilbur Gingrich, William F. Arendt, Frederick W. Danker, editors. *A Greek-English Lexicon of the New Testament and Other Early Christian Literature*. 2nd ed. Chicago: University of Chicago Press, 1979.
Becker, Ernest. *The Denial of Death*. New York: Free Press, 1974.
Beker, J. Christiaan. *Paul the Apostle: The Triumph of God in Life and Thought*. Minneapolis: Fortress, 1980.
———. *Suffering and Hope: The Biblical Vision and the Human Predicament*. Grand Rapids: Eerdmans, 1994.
———. *The Triumph of God: The Essence of Paul's Thought*. Minneapolis: Fortress, 1990.
Billman, Kathleen D., and Daniel L. Migliore. *Rachel's Cry: Prayer of Lament and Rebirth of Hope*. Cleveland: United Church Press, 1999.
Birch, Bruce, "Biblical Faith and the Loss of Children." *Christian Century* (1983).
Black, Kathy. *A Healing Homiletic: Preaching and Disability*. Nashville: Abingdon, 1996.
———. "A Perspective of the Disabled." In *Preaching Justice: Ethnic and Cultural Perspectives*, edited by Christine Marie Smith. Cleveland: United Church Press, 1998.
Bombeck, Erma. "When Does One Reach Age of Freedom to Eat?" *The Telegraph* (Nashua, New Hampshire), March 17, 1989, p. 40.
Boys, Mary C. "The Cross: Should a Symbol Betrayed Be Reclaimed?" *Cross Currents* 44 (1994) 17.
Brown, Sally A., and Patrick D. Miller. *Lament: Recovering Practices in Pulpit, Pew, and Public Square*. Louisville: Westminster John Knox, 2005.
Brueggemann, Walter. *The Message of the Psalms*. Minneapolis: Fortress, 1985.
Buechner, Frederick. *Speak What We Feel (Not What We Ought to Say): Four Who Wrote in Blood*. New York: Harper & Row, 2004.
———. *Telling the Truth: The Gospel as Tragedy, Comedy, and Fairy Tale*. New York: Harper & Row, 1977.

Bibliography

Bornkamm, Gunter. "Mysterion." In *The Theological Dictionary of the New Testament*, edited by Gerhard Kittel, translated and edited by Geoffrey W. Bromiley, vol. 4. Grand Rapids: Eerdmans, 1967.

Brown, Alexandra. *The Cross and Human Transformation: Paul's Apocalyptic Word in 1 Corinthians*. Minneapolis: Fortress, 1995.

Burgess, Katherine. "Report: Church giving reaches Depression-era record lows." *Religion News Service*, October 24, 2013. Online: http://www.religionnews.com/2013/10/24/report-church-giving-reaches-depression-era-record-lows/.

Buttrick, David. *Homiletic: Moves and Structures*. Minneapolis: Augsburg Fortress, 1987.

Campbell, Charles. *The Word Before the Powers*. Louisville: Westminster John Knox, 2002.

Callimachi, Rukmini. "ISIS Enshrines a Theology of Rape." *New York Times*, August 13, 2015. Online: http://www.nytimes.com/2015/08/14/world/middleeast/isis-enshrines-a-theology-of-rape.html.

Davidson, Robert. *The Courage to Doubt*. Norwich: Hymns Ancient and Modern, 2012.

Eliot, T. S. *The Four Quartets*. Boston: Mariner, 1968.

Eusebius. *Life of Constantine*. In vol. 1 of *A Select Library of the Nicene and Post-Nicene Fathers of the Christian Church*, 2nd series, edited by Philip Schaff and Henry Wace. Grand Rapids: Eerdmans, 1952.

Farley, Edward. *Practicing Gospel: Unconventional Thoughts on the Church's Ministry*. Louisville: Westminster John Knox, 2003.

Gadamer, Hans Georg. *Truth and Method*. 2nd rev. ed. New York: Continuum, 2004.

Goizuez, Roberto S. *Caminemo Con Jesús: Toward a Hispanic/Latino Theology of Accompaniment*. Maryknoll, NY: Orbis, 1995.

Gorman, Michael J. *Cruciformity: Paul's Narrative Spirituality of the Cross*. Grand Rapids: Eerdmans, 2001.

Gunkel, Hermann. *Einleitung in die Psalmen: Die Gattungen der Religiosen Lyrik Israels (Zwelte Auflage)*. Gottingen: Vandenhoeck and Ruprecht, 1966.

Heim, S. Mark. *Saved from Sacrifice: A Theology of the Cross*. Grand Rapids: Eerdmans, 2006.

Heschel, Abraham. *The Prophets*. Peabody, MA: Hendrickson, 2007.

Hilkert, Mary Catherine. *Naming Grace: Preaching and the Sacramental Imagination*. New York: Continuum, 1997.

———. "Preaching the Folly of the Cross." *Word and World* 19 (1999) 40.

Hogan, Lucy Lind, and Robert Reid. *Connecting with the Congregation: Rhetoric and the Art of Preaching*. Nashville: Abingdon, 1999.

Howard, Alton. *Songs of Faith and Praise*. West Monroe, LA: Howard Pub., 1994.

Irving, John. *A Prayer for Owen Meany*. New York: Harper, 2012.

Johnson, Stephen. *Apocalyptic Eschatology as Homiletical Deep Structure*. ThD diss., University of Toronto, 2007.

Kay, James F. *Preaching and Theology*. St. Louis: Chalice, 2007.

Keillor, Garrison. *Lake Wobegon U.S.A.* Audio recording of narratives from the radio program *A Prairie Home Companion*. St. Paul, MN: HighBridge, 1993.

Kelsey, David. *The Uses of Scripture in Recent Theology*. Philadelphia: Fortress, 1976.

Kenneson, Philip, and James Street. *Selling Out the Church in the Marketplace of Desire: The Dangers of Church Marketing*. Nashville: Abingdon, 1997.

Kierkegaard, Soren. *Parables of Kierkegaard*. Edited by Thomas C. Oden. Princeton: Princeton University Press, 1978.

Bibliography

King, Martin Luther, Jr. *A Testament of Hope: The Essential Writings and Speeches of Martin Luther King, Jr.* Edited by James M. Washington. New York: HarperOne, 2003.

Knowles, Michael P. *We Preach Not Ourselves: Paul on Proclamation.* Grand Rapids: Brazos, 2008.

Kottler, Jeffrey A. "What REALLY Leads to Change in People's Lives?" *Psychology Today*, Change, July 24, 2013. Online: https://www.psychologytoday.com/blog/change/201307/what-really-leads-change-in-people-s-lives.

Kuruvilla, Abraham. "The World in Front of the Text: An Intermediary Between Text and Praxis." Unpublished paper presented for the Homiletics and Biblical Studies section at the 2008 Society of Biblical Literature annual convention, Boston.

Long, Thomas G. *The Witness of Preaching.* Louisville: Westminster/John Knox, 1989.

Lucian. *On Salaried Posts in Great Houses.* Translated by A. M. Harmon. Loeb Classical Library. New York: Putnam, 1921.

Marcus, Joel. *Mark 8–18.* Anchor Yale Bible. New Haven, CT: Yale University Press, 2009.

Marlin, Randal. *Propaganda and the Ethics of Persuasion.* Orchard Park, NY: Broadview, 2002.

Martin, Luther H. *Hellenistic Religions: An Introduction.* New York: Oxford University Press, 1987.

Martyn, J. Louis. "Epistemology at the Turn of the Ages: 2 Corinthians 5:16." In *Christian History and Interpretation: Studies Presented to John Knox,* edited by W. R. Farmer, C. F. D. Moule, and R. R. Niebuhr. Cambridge: Cambridge University Press, 1967.

McCann, Forrest M., editor. *Great Songs of the Church.* Abilene, TX: ACU Press, 1986.

Meyer, Marvin W., editor. *The Ancient Mysteries: A Sourcebook: Sacred Texts of the Mystery Religions of the Ancient Mediterranean World.* San Francisco: Harper & Row, 1987.

Mitchell, Henry. *Black Preaching: The Recovery of a Powerful Art.* Nashville: Abingdon, 1990.

Morse, Christopher. *Not Every Spirit: The Dogmatics of Disbelief.* 2nd ed. London: T. & T. Clark, 2009.

Muehl, William. "The Cult of the Publican." In, *A Chorus of Witnesses: Model Sermons for Today's Preacher,* edited by Cornelius Plantinga and Thomas G. Long. Grand Rapids: Eerdmans, 1994.

Nouwen, Henri. *A Letter of Consolation.* New York: HarperCollins, 2009.

Peterson, Brian K. *Eloquence and the Proclamation of the Gospel in Corinth.* Atlanta: Scholars, 1998.

Powery, Luke. *Dem Dry Bones: Preaching, Death, and Hope.* Minneapolis: Fortress, 2012.

———. *Spirit Speech: Lament and Celebration in Preaching.* Minneapolis: Fortress, 2009.

Reid, Robert S., editor. *Slow of Speech and Unclean Lips: Contemporary Images of Preaching Identity.* Eugene, OR: Wipf & Stock, 2010.

Resner, André. *Just Preaching: Prophetic Voices for Economic Justice.* St. Louis: Chalice, 2003.

———. *Preacher and Cross: Person and Message in Theology and Rhetoric.* Grand Rapids: Eerdmans, 1999.

———. "Social Justice." In *The New Interpreter's Handbook of Preaching,* edited by Paul Scott Wilson. Nashville: Abingdon, 2008.

Reumann, John. "'Servants of God'—Pre-Christian Religious Application of the *Oikonomos* in Greek." *Journal of Biblical Literature* 77 (1958) 339–49.

———. "*Oikonomia*-Terms in Paul in Comparison with Lucan *Heilsgeschichte*." *New Testament Studies* 13 (1966/67) 147–67.

Bibliography

Ricoeur, Paul. *The Symbolism of Evil*. Translated by Emerson Buchanan. Boston: Beacon, 1967.

Sampley, J. Paul. *Walking Between the Times: Paul's Moral Reasoning*. Minneapolis: Fortress, 1991.

Soelle, Dorothée. *Suffering*. Minneapolis: Fortress, 1984.

Thomas, Frank. *They Like to Never Quit Praisin' God: The Role of Celebration in Preaching*. Cleveland: Pilgrim, 1997.

Tracy, David. *The Analogical Imagination: Christian Theology and the Culture of Pluralism*. New York: Crossroad, 1981.

Tripolitis, Antonia. *Religions of the Hellenistic-Roman Age*. Grand Rapids: Eerdmans, 2002.

Weaver, J. Denny. *The Non-Violent Atonement*. 2nd ed. Grand Rapids: Eerdmans, 2011.

Wiesel, Elie. *Night*. Translated by Stella Rodway. New York: Bantam, 1960.

———. *Zalman, or, The Madness of God*. New York: Random House, 1974.

Wilson, Paul Scott. *Setting Words on Fire: Putting God at the Center of the Sermon*. Nashville: Abingdon, 2008.

———. *The Four Pages of the Sermon*. Nashville: Abingdon, 1999.

Wolterstorff, Nicholas. *Lament for a Son*. Grand Rapids: Eerdmans, 1987.

Wood, Charles. *Vision and Discernment: An Orientation to Theological Study*. Atlanta: Scholars, 1985.

www.ingramcontent.com/pod-product-compliance
Lightning Source LLC
Chambersburg PA
CBHW072153160426
43197CB00012B/2370